The LORD said to Moses,
"Speak to the Israelites and say to them:
'These are my appointed festivals,
the appointed festivals of the LORD,
which you are to proclaim as
sacred assemblies.'"

LEVITICUS 23:1-2

THE BIBLICAL FESTIVALS
ימועדי מקרא

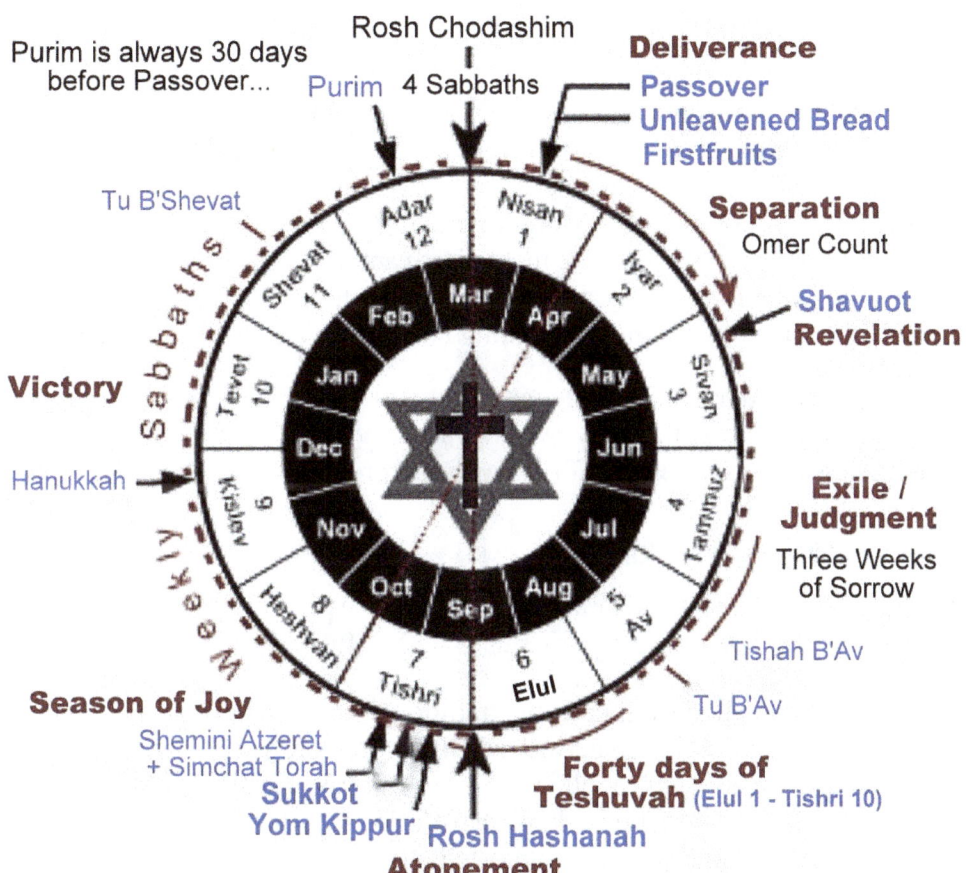

including

פסח סדר ההגדה בכתובים

A PASSOVER SEDER
The Haggadah in Scripture

ABOUT DR. BILL MOREHOUSE

Dr. Morehouse was raised in a traditional Christian home in the 1950's and functionally became a humanist during college and medical school in the 1960's. After completing his medical residency in Family Medicine in the early 1970's he embarked on a career of serving the poor but soon found that his secular faith and alternative lifestyle were woefully inadequate to the task.

In 1974 he underwent a dramatic conversion from the philosophy and lifestyle he had been living to a wholehearted commitment to Jesus as his LORD and Savior. After returning to medicine and marrying in 1975, he and his wife dedicated themselves to growing in faith, raising their family of four children (now with spouses and grandchildren), and providing Christ-centered service to some of the most disadvantaged members of their community. During this time he and his family developed a strong love, not only for God and one another but for God's entire family, including His chosen people and our shared heritage.

Since retiring from active clinical practice in July 2018, Dr. Morehouse has been devoted to continued Christian growth, study, writing, and teaching about the Kingdom of God. He has had long personal experience with the material presented.

The Biblical Festivals, including A Passover Seder

Copyright 2021 by William R. Morehouse
ISBN: 979-8-9850767-1-4 (paperback)

This material was compiled from multiple traditional sources and woven together with original commentary and selected additional Bible references. The Seder Haggadah was designed to be used at home, in small groups, or with larger gatherings to celebrate the Passover. Cover illustration "The Light of the World" by Alex Levin (www.artlevin.com) used by permission. Unless otherwise indicated, all Scripture quotations are from The ESV Bible® (The Holy Bible, English Standard Version®), copyright © 2001 by Crossway, a publishing ministry of Good News Publishers. Used by permission, All rights reserved.

His Kingdom Press
Rochester, New York 14619

Special discounts are available on quantity purchases by associations, educators, and others. For details, contact the publisher through www.hiskingdom.us/press.

THE BIBLICAL FESTIVALS

A Lively and Prophetic Heritage 1
The Root and the Branches.. 3
God's Festivals in the Scriptures.. 4
The Jewish Calendar 6
    Shabbat or The Sabbath Day – A Weekly Feast 8
    1. Pesach or Passover – Nisan 14-15 9
    2. Chag HaMotzi or Unleavened Bread – Nisan 15-22 10
    3. Reshit Katzir or Bikkurim/Firstfruits – Nisan 16-17 10
    4. Shavuot or Pentecost – Sivan 6-7 11
        Tisha B'Av and the 40 Days of Teshuvah – Av 9 and Elul 1 12
    5. Rosh Hashanah or Jewish New Year – Tishri 1-2.......................................13
    6. Yom Kippur or Day of Atonement – Tishri 10..14
    7. Sukkot or The Feast of Tabernacles – Tishri 15-22 16
        Shemini Atzeret, Simchat Torah, Hanukkah, Tu B'Shevat 17
        Purim or The Festival of Lots – Adar 14...20
Jesus or Yeshua?..23

A PASSOVER SEDER

Background 28
Preparations and The Seder Table..30
    Lighting the Candles...32
    1. Kadesh – The Sanctification 33
    2. Urchatz – Cleansing the Hands 34
    3. Karpas – Eating the Greens..34
    4. Yachatz – Breaking the Matzah 35
    5. Maggid – Recitation of the Service 37
    6. Rachtzah – The Cleansing 42
    7. Motzi – Giving Thanks for Bread..44
    8. Matzo – Eating the Matzah 44
    9. Maror – Tasting the Bitter Herb...44
    10. Korech – A Reminder of the Temple 44
    11. Shulchan Orech – The Passover Meal 45
    12. Tzafun – Eating the Afikoman..46
    13. Berach – Grace 47
    14. Hallel – Praise the LORD 50
    15. Nirtzah – The Acceptance 52
Chad Gadya – An Only Kid song..53
Traditional Passover Recipes and Notes...54
Jesus fulfills the Promise of Passover 58
Jewish Holidays 2022-26, References, and Endnotes 60

ACKNOWLEDGEMENTS

The work you have in your hands is a compilation of words, phrases, sentences, and even modestly larger fragments of written material contributed by many, many writers extending back from today's world of faith into ancient times. The only thing that I offer as my contribution is the matrix of words that holds the various parts together in the chronological and thematic order in which I have assembled them.

Let me use two Hebrew words associated with how Passover is celebrated, *Seder* (סדר) and *Haggadah* (הההגדה), to explain the kind of collaborative heritage that I have attempted to share. Seder means arrangement or "order" and refers to the outline of events and readings that has developed for the annual Passover celebration mandated in Leviticus. The Haggadah is the guide book participants use into which the Seder order has been assembled using both traditional and non-traditional readings.

Who wrote the Haggadah? Well, over the years it has been gathered and modified and copied from a host of sources, and its core contents can be found in books and on the Internet in a variety of forms. What you will find in this small book will be both unique and yet familiar to many of you, kind of like a wedding celebration that has gathered something old, something new, something borrowed, and something blue…

The first half of the compendium in your hands follows the traditional Jewish calendar and descriptions in presenting the Sabbath and 7 Biblical festivals outlined in Leviticus 23 as well as 7 additional commemorations foreshadowed in other Scriptural passages. I would like to gratefully acknowledge the multiple sources I have consulted and sometimes copied from shamelessly in assembling a concise and faithful introduction to this vital part of our shared Biblical heritage. I sincerely hope that you will be inspired to research each festival in greater depth for unfolding evidences of His divine and messianic plan of redemption as your love for God, His Word, His people, and the community of mankind grows.

The contemporary Haggadah for celebrating the Passover Seder included in the second half of the book carries forward all the traditional elements in its outline, components, instructions, and prayers. In addition, and in harmony with the tradition of keeping our Haggadah fresh and relevant, we have enhanced its timeless format with Scripture verses, songs, and other materials that support the underlying theme of Pesach.

I am particularly grateful to the scholarly work of so many individuals and organizations as well as to inspired contributors in our local fellowship and beyond. I would especially like to honor my wife and life partner, Susan, for her unfailing love and support over the decades we have been given to share life, faith, family, and community together.

Dr. Bill Morehouse
Sukkot 5782 – September 2021

A LIVELY AND PROPHETIC HERITAGE

Why are we carefully examining and honoring something as old, and arguably outdated, as the festivals of ancient Israel? For many Christians the question has to do with the "Law of Moses" (the *Torat Moshe* or תורה משה in Hebrew) of the Pentateuch, which records God's instructions about the annual festivals in Leviticus 23 among a host of other teachings. "What do we have to do with the Law?" they ask. Jesus addressed the subject directly during the Sermon on the Mount:

> *Do not think that I have come to abolish the Law or the Prophets; I have not come to abolish them but to fulfill them. For truly, I say to you, until heaven and earth pass away, not an iota, not a dot, will pass from the Law until all is accomplished. Therefore whoever relaxes one of the least of these commandments and teaches others to do the same will be called least in the kingdom of heaven, but whoever does them and teaches them will be called great in the kingdom of heaven.*
> Matthew 5:17-19

It's crucial to understand that Biblical "Law" (תורה) is not "law" in our modern sense of the word but a set of authoritative instructions and teachings given to us by our loving God to enhance, guide, improve, and safeguard our lives. Only when we shift out of grace mode by turning His "Law" into a legalistic set of rules and regulations do we lose the blessing and get entangled in binding complications. What, then, has God called us to do as we reach out to love and honor Him? Simply listen and seek to understand, follow, and obey Him as cheerfully and gratefully as His Spirit enables us.

> *Trust in the LORD with all your heart, and do not lean on your own understanding. In all your ways acknowledge him, and he will make straight your paths.*
> Proverbs 3:5-6

Then we can reap the blessings! Unfortunately, somewhere along the line we've made things very complicated and thrown out a lot of the blessings. One of the big blessings lost was our love for one another, including Christians for their Jewish spiritual forebears. Antisemitism found a home in the separated Gentile church and we lost our heritage and a vital part of our prophetic vision. Paul expressed it clearly:

> *I am speaking the truth in Christ – I am not lying; my conscience bears me witness in the Holy Spirit – that I have great sorrow and unceasing anguish in my heart. For I could wish that I myself were accursed and cut off from Christ for the sake of my brothers, my kinsmen according to the flesh. They are Israelites, and to them belong the adoption, the glory, the covenants, the giving of the law, the worship, and the promises. To them belong the patriarchs, and from their race, according to the flesh, is the Christ, who is God over all, blessed forever. Amen.*
> Romans 9:1-5

> *I ask, then, has God rejected his people? By no means! For I myself am an Israelite, a descendant of Abraham, a member of the tribe of Benjamin. God has not rejected his*

people whom he foreknew. Do you not know what the Scripture says of Elijah, how he appeals to God against Israel? "LORD, they have killed your prophets, they have demolished your altars, and I alone am left, and they seek my life." But what is God's reply to him? "I have kept for myself seven thousand men who have not bowed the knee to Baal." So too at the present time there is a remnant, chosen by grace. But if it is by grace, it is no longer on the basis of works; otherwise grace would no longer be grace.

Romans 11:1-6

Lest you be wise in your own sight, I do not want you to be unaware of this mystery, brothers: a partial hardening has come upon Israel, until the fullness of the Gentiles has come in. And in this way all Israel will be saved, as it is written,

> *"The Deliverer will come from Zion; he will banish ungodliness from Jacob; and this will be my covenant with them when I take away their sins."*

As regards the gospel, they are enemies for your sake. But as regards election, they are beloved for the sake of their forefathers. For the gifts and the calling of God are irrevocable. For just as you were at one time disobedient to God but now have received mercy because of their disobedience, so they too have now been disobedient in order that by the mercy shown to you they also may now receive mercy. For God has consigned all to disobedience, that he may have mercy on all.

Oh, the depth of the riches and wisdom and knowledge of God! How unsearchable are his judgments and how inscrutable his ways!

Romans 11:25-33

As Isaiah prophesied so many years ago,

All we like sheep have gone astray; we have turned – every one – to his own way; and the LORD has laid on him the iniquity of us all.

Isaiah 53:6

The time is here to open our hearts, turn back to our God and one another, and receive His forgiveness, guidance, and blessing.

Faithful celebration of the Biblical Festivals calls for study and understanding. The goal of this book is to provide a simple introduction and cultural bridge. Several references are listed at the back for further study that will add essential details about each festival's background and ideas for how to benefit even more from the experience.

Probably the best way to grow and learn is to reach across the religious and cultural divide that has come between us as Christian and Jewish people to seek and find reconciliation in our hearts as we rediscover our shared spiritual history. Our God will supply all our needs according to His riches in glory! Let's start now by reaching out to our spiritual family and finding out what He has for us in the festivals He's given us. Brothers and sisters, please believe me when I report that God's plans include one wonderful celebration of His love after another all through the year!

The Biblical Festivals מועדי מקראי

THE ROOT AND THE BRANCHES
He is the Vine and we are His Branches

Now I am speaking to you Gentiles. Inasmuch then as I am an apostle to the Gentiles, I magnify my ministry in order somehow to make my fellow Jews jealous, and thus save some of them. For if their rejection means the reconciliation of the world, what will their acceptance mean but life from the dead? If the dough offered as firstfruits is holy, so is the whole lump, and if the root is holy, so are the branches.

But if some of the branches were broken off, and you, although a wild olive shoot, were grafted in among the others and now share in the nourishing root of the olive tree, do not be arrogant toward the branches. If you are, remember it is not you who support the root, but the root that supports you.   Romans 11.13-18

A Timetable

We in the western world have been raised in a culture dominated by a post-Constantinian worldview of time and Christian faith, rather than one that is biblically Hebrew or even completely faithful to Scriptural understandings shared in both Testaments, Old and New. Our days begin and end at midnight, rather than the biblical breaking point of sunset. Our days are named after celestial bodies and Norse gods revered in pagan worship and our work week begins on Monday and ends with a day of rest on Sunday (the first day of the week), rather than continuing the biblical pattern that Jesus and His disciples adhered to of keeping Sabbath on the seventh day.

Our Gregorian calendar years are numbered from the birth of Christ, rather than from the traditional Hebrew reckoning of the beginning of creation. And we have replaced the biblically instituted feasts of Passover, Shavuot, Rosh Hashanah, Yom Kippur, and Sukkot celebrated by the people of Israel with a variety of newly-minted Christian seasons like Advent and Lent and holy days like Christmas and Easter, as well as secular and neo-pagan holidays (holy days?) like New Year's Day, Memorial Day, Independence Day, Labor Day, Halloween, and Thanksgiving.

Rediscovering the worldview and timeframe of our Hebrew heritage points us toward and allows us to more fully appreciate the activities of Jesus of Nazareth as the promised messiah at the time of His birth, earthly ministry, crucifixion, death, resurrection, ascension, and the promised outpouring of the Holy Spirit that followed. And, in keeping with the format of all of the festivals, each celebration helps us recall the past, rejoice in the present, and look forward to the future in faith as we anticipate the coming of the Messiah to establish His Kingdom in our midst.

GOD'S FESTIVALS מועדי IN THE SCRIPTURES

The LORD said to Moses, "Speak to the Israelites and say to them: 'These are my appointed festivals, the appointed festivals of the LORD, which you are to proclaim as sacred assemblies…at their appointed times.'"   Leviticus 23:1-2, 4 (NIV)

There are numerous references throughout the entire Bible to the festivals (sacred gatherings or "appointed times" in Hebrew) that God set aside for regular celebration, consecration, rest, and worship as noted in the list drawn from Leviticus 23 below:

	Biblical Festival	Leviticus	New Testament
	Shabbat	23:3	Multiple references
A	**1. Pesach** **Passover**	23:5	Matthew 26:2, 17-19 Mark 14:12-16 Luke 2:41-42; 22:1, 7-20 John 2:13, 23; 6:4; 13:1-30 Acts 20:6 1 Corinthians 11:23-29
A	**2. Chag HaMotzi** **Unleavened Bread**	23:6-8	1 Corinthians 5:6-8
A	**3. Reshit Katzir** **Firstfruits**	23:10-14	Observed as Easter
B	**4. Shavuot** **Feast of Weeks** or **Pentecost**	23:15-22	Acts 2:1-21; 20:16 1 Corinthians 16:8
C	**5. Rosh Hashanah** **Feast of Trumpets**	23:23-25	Matthew 24:30-31 1 Thessalonians 4:16-17 Revelation 11:15
C	**6. Yom Kippur** **Day of Atonement**	23:26-32	Acts 27:9, Hebrews 9
C	**7. Sukkot** **Feast of Tabernacles**	23:33-43	John 7:1-2, 7:8, 10, 14

The major festivals outlined above and discussed in the first half of our book are those designated by God for regular observance which have either been variably carried over with modifications or set aside entirely by the wider Christian community. The first of these, although technically not a festival in the sense that the others are, is the weekly Sabbath day set aside as the 4th Commandment in Exodus 20:8-11 to be kept faithfully on the seventh day. Most people in our modern world have retained some relationship with the concept if not the actual practice of keeping Sabbath.

The remaining seven have been clustered as three annual Pilgrimage Festivals which include A) the spring celebration of Passover (along with the Feasts of Unleavened Bread and Firstfruits), followed by B) Shavuot or Pentecost, and then C) the fall celebrations of Rosh Hashanah (Trumpets), Yom Kippur (the Day of Atonement), and Sukkot (the Feast of Tabernacles). We have included five more celebrations commonly observed in the Jewish community that have less directive Biblical origins, including Shemini Atzeret, Simchat Torah, Hanukkah, Tu B'Shevat, and the popular Purim festivities.

Of the Pilgrimage Festivals, the two that most Christians are familiar with are the those of Passover which transitioned into a set of observances from Palm Sunday to Easter Sunday, and the Shavuot festival which Christians celebrate as Pentecost in remembrance of the outpouring of the Holy Spirit on the disciples gathered in the Upper Room following the reported crucifixion, resurrection, and ascension of Jesus. Some of the core sentiments of the third Pilgrimage Festival (encompassing the fall holidays or "holy days" of Rosh Hashanah, Yom Kippur, and Sukkot) may be found in Lenten activities. However, unlike the first two Festivals, Sukkot is a forward-looking celebration that remains to be fulfilled when the Messiah comes to establish His millennial reign as prophesied in Zechariah 14.

Jesus and His disciples celebrated all of the prescribed feasts. What can both Christians and Jews learn today from the Bible, the festivals, each other, and the example of those who have gone before us? Why did God set things up and instruct His people to carry them out the way He did? Who are His people in our world? Are we listening and being obedient to His voice?

In the second half of our book we have expanded upon and showcased Passover because it is the cornerstone of our mutual salvation and redemption, a celebration of the faithfulness of God in saving those who called upon His Name and obeyed His voice during the Exodus as well as all who have called on His name for salvation from the slavery of sin ever since. The Bible is united in its witness to the God who saves, sanctifies, and sends His people back out into the world as redeemed citizens and ambassadors of His Kingdom on earth. Please join us as we learn to celebrate our common heritage together.

Blessed are those who wash their festal robes, so that they may have the right to the tree of life and that they may enter the city by the gates.   Revelation 22:14

קהילת עץ החיים
The Tree of Life Community

THE JEWISH CALENDAR
A traditional Biblical approach to reckoning time

Years

The Jewish year nominally starts on the first day of the month of Tishri when the Levitical celebration of Rosh Hashanah, "the Head of the Year," takes place. According to tradition, this is the day indicated by Scriptural calculations that God made Adam and Eve as the capstone of His creation of our universe and yields a number equivalent to the age of the world. To find the corresponding Jewish year for any year on the Gregorian calendar, add 3760 to the Gregorian number if it is before Rosh Hashanah or 3761 if it is after.

Months

Our Biblical charts and lists of festivals always start with Nisan as the first month of the year, however, as God instructed Moses when Passover was instituted:

> *This month shall be for you the beginning of months... the first month of the year for you.*
>
> Exodus 12:2

Months in the Jewish calendar are based on lunar cycles. Towards the beginning of the moon's cycle, it appears as a thin crescent. That is the signal for a new Jewish month. The moon grows until it is full in the middle of the month, and then it begins to wane until it cannot be seen. It remains invisible for approximately two days and then the thin crescent reappears and the cycle begins again.

The entire lunar cycle takes approximately 29½ days. Since a month needs to consist of complete days, a month is sometimes twenty-nine days long, and sometimes thirty. To keep the Jewish calendar synchronized with the seasons, a leap month called "Adar 2" as listed at the bottom of the following chart is inserted in "leap years" during seven of every nineteen years based on barley harvest times in Israel.

The first day of the month, as well as the thirtieth day of a long month, is called Rosh Chodesh (ראש חודש or the "Head of the Month") and has semi-festive status. Knowing exactly when the month begins has always been important in Jewish practice, because the Torah schedules the Jewish festivals according to the days of the month.

Dates of Holidays

The story is told that one man in a synagogue was overheard to ask another, "When is Hanukkah this year?" The other man smiled slyly and replied, "Same as always: the 25th of Kislev." This humorous comment makes an important point: the date of Jewish holidays does not change from year to year. Holidays are celebrated on the same day of the Jewish calendar every year, but the Jewish year is not the same length as a solar year on the CE calendar used by most of the western world, so the date shifts on the civil calendar. You will find a chart of the exact Gregorian calendar dates of the major Jewish holidays from 2022 through 2026 CE along with suggestions for further study on pages 60-64.

The Biblical Festivals   מועדי מקראי

The Jewish calendar's months with associated holidays:

Hebrew Month		Holiday Dates	Length	Gregorian
נִיסָן	1. Nisan	The New Year for Jewish Kings is celebrated on Nisan 1; On Nisan 14-15 Passover starts, followed by Unleavened Bread on Nisan15-22 with Reshit Katzir in the midst	30 days	March-April
אִיָּיר	2. Iyar	Lag B'Omer on Iyar 19 is the 33rd day of the Counting of the Omer	29 days	April-May
סִיוָן	3. Sivan	Shavuot commemorates the giving of the Law on Sivan 6-7, 50 days ("Pentecost") after Passover.	30 days	May-June
תַּמּוּז	4. Tammuz		29 days	June-July
אָב	5. Av	Tisha B'Av (the 9th of Av) commemorates historical Jewish tragedies.	30 days	July-August
אֱלוּל	6. Elul	New Year for Animals and the 40 days of Teshuvah start on Elul 1.	29 days	August-September
תִּשְׁרֵי	7. Tishri	Rosh Hashanah (New Year for People) and Yom Kippur (The High Holidays), Sukkot, Shmini Atzeret, and Simchat Torah.	30 days	September-October
חֶשְׁוָן	8. Cheshvan		29 or 30 days	October-November
כִּסְלֵו	9. Kislev	Hanukkah celebrations start on Kislev 25.	30 or 29 days	November-December
טֵבֵת	10. Tevet	Conclusion of Hanukkah.	29 days	December-January
שְׁבָט	11. Shevat	Tu B'Shevat (New Year of the Trees) or Jewish Arbor Day.	30 days	January-February
אֲדָר	12. Adar (in non-leap years)	Purim (The Feast of Lots) celebrated on Adar 14.	30 days	February-March
אֲדָר א אֲדָר ב	12. Adar I or Aleph and 13. Adar II or Bet (leap years)	Purim celebrated in Adar II in leap years.	29 days	February-March

God's Appointed Times

SHABBAT שבת

A Weekly Day of Rest

God called the light Day, and the darkness he called Night. And there was evening and there was morning, the first day... And on the seventh day God finished his work that he had done, and he rested on the seventh day from all his work that he had done. So God blessed the seventh day and made it holy, because on it God rested from all his work that he had done in creation.

Genesis 1:5; 2:1-3

Six days shall work be done, but on the seventh day is a Sabbath of solemn rest, a holy convocation. You shall do no work. It is a Sabbath to the LORD in all your dwelling places.

Leviticus 23:3

According to the account in Genesis, when God created time He first created night and then day, which makes sense because there must first be darkness before light can penetrate it. While a day in the secular calendar arbitrarily begins and ends at midnight, a Jewish day goes from nightfall to nightfall. The weekly Sabbath or Shabbat begins on Friday evening, and on those dates where certain activities are restricted – such as working on Shabbat or major holidays – the restrictions go into effect the same evening, except for most fast days which begin at sunrise the following morning.

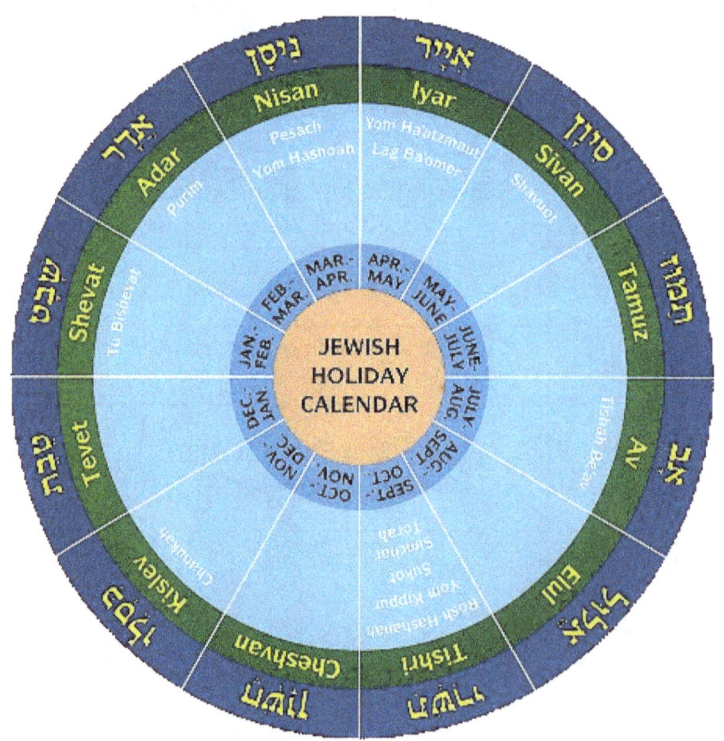

PASSOVER פסח and THE SEDER סדר
Our Jewish-Christian Haggadah ההגדה

> *"In the first month, on the fourteenth day of the month at twilight, is the LORD's Passover."*
>
> Leviticus 23:5

Passover (פסח), perhaps the oldest and most preeminent of the Jewish Pilgrim Festivals, is based on the *Hag HaPesach* observances of ancient Israel (see Page 28). These were preserved primarily in Exodus 12-14 as celebrations of remembrance of God's deliverance of His people from slavery in Egypt. Although the preceding chart refers to Rosh Hashanah (which means "the Head of the Year" in Hebrew) as one of four designated Jewish New Years (this one for People), the month of Nisan in which Passover takes place is identified as the first month of the New Year for the year as a whole and, more specifically, for Jewish Kings:

> *"This month shall be for you the beginning of months. It shall be the first month of the year for you. ... This day shall be for you a memorial day, and you shall keep it as a feast to the LORD; throughout your generations you shall observe it as an ordinance forever."*
>
> Exodus 12.2, 14

The term Passover refers to the tenth and final plague God brought upon the Egyptians to persuade Pharaoh to let the people go, the death of all the firstborn of Egypt. In obedience to God's instructions, those who believed placed the blood of a lamb on the door posts of their homes, so that God would "*pass over*" those homes. The festival actually celebrates the entire sequence of events that led the Israelites' from slavery to freedom.

While based in those Biblical events, the celebration encompasses much more as it becomes a vehicle to celebrate the very nature of God and His gracious work in the world. It is in this larger context that Jesus (ישוע) fulfilled and transformed the Passover service into a demonstration of God's new work of deliverance in the Messiah (המשיח), allowing believers in Christ to celebrate this ancient festival with even deeper meaning.

Much more detail about Passover and its celebration can be found in the history, Seder preparations, and Haggadah presented in the latter half of this book.

God's Appointed Times

CHAG HAMOTZI חג המוצי
The Feast of Unleavened Bread

"On the fifteenth day of that month [Nisan] the LORD's Festival of Unleavened Bread begins; for seven days you must eat bread made without yeast. On the first day hold a sacred assembly and do no regular work. For seven days present a food offering to the LORD. And on the seventh day hold a sacred assembly and do no regular work."

Leviticus 23:6-8

The week starting with and immediately following Pesach or Passover is dedicated to the personal and corporate discipline and symbolic purification of the Feast of Unleavened Bread. It commemorates the flight of all those who heeded Moses' warning, gathered up their bread dough for the journey before it had risen (unleavened), and left Egypt after death "passed them over" the night before. Symbolically, they were leaving behind "the leaven of the Egyptians" – all the sinful ways that their lives had become entangled in the world – and heading by faith for a Promised Land yet to be revealed.

Celebrating this feast is a good reminder, not only of God's grace in calling us out of darkness into His light but that it's a God-sized job to get the world's "leaven" out of the lives of slaves like us.

RESHIT KATZIR קציר ראשית or BIKKURIM ביכורים
The Feast of Firstfruits

Speak to the people of Israel and say to them, "When you come into the land that I give you and reap its harvest, you shall bring the sheaf of the firstfruits of your harvest to the priest, and he shall wave the sheaf before the LORD, so that you may be accepted. On the day after the Sabbath [that follows Passover] the priest shall wave it."

Leviticus 23:10-11

The day after the first regular Sabbath during the Feast of Unleavened Bread in the week immediately following Passover is set aside in Leviticus to celebrate *Reshit Katzir* (Hebrew for "firstfruits" of the barley harvest) representing the bounty of God's provision in the Promised Land. Many in the Jewish community celebrate on the second day of Pesach.

The closest thing to the Feast of Firstfruits that the Christian community observes would be the festivities of Easter (named for Ishtar, the pagan goddess of fertility). At this time Christians celebrate Christ's resurrection as the "firstfruits" from the dead on the first day of the week (Sunday) following His Last Supper, the Passover Seder meal that Jesus shared with His disciples, saying "Do this in remembrance of Me," before being crucified as our Passover lamb. The sequence is perfect, since Resurrection Day was Reshit Katzir that year (see "Jesus fulfills the promise of Passover" chart on Pages 58-59).

The Biblical Festivals   מועדי מקרא

SHAVUOT שבועות or PENTECOST
The Feast of Weeks

Shavuot is the Hebrew word for "weeks" and refers to the Biblical "Feast of Weeks" which marks the giving of the Torah at Mount Sinai seven weeks after Israel's exodus from Egypt. Since *Sefirat HaOmer* or the Counting of the Omer (עֹמֶר or "sheaves" of the barley harvest) begins on the Sabbath just before Reshit Katzir, Shavuot takes place exactly 50 days after the first regular Sabbath during the Feast of Unleavened Bread. The Shavuot festival is also referred to as Pentecost (based on the Greek word for "fifty) and is celebrated on the seventh Sunday after Easter in the Christian community.

Origins

As noted above, the development of Shavuot was founded on an ancient Canaanite summer festival, long celebrated by the Israelites, which marked the beginning of the wheat harvest seven weeks after the firstfruits of barley had been harvested. God's timely fulfillment during the exodus set aside the ancient festival as a major "appointed time."

The Giving of the Law

50 days after crossing the Red Sea during their precipitous departure from Egypt, which included stops at Marah, Elim, and Rephidim, the Israelites' arrived at Mount Sinai where Moses received the 10 Commandments of the Torah. Then, after staying on the mountain for 40 days and in the plains below during the remaining 9 months of the first year, he received further detailed guidelines about the Tabernacle of Meeting, priestly rituals, and a host of behavioral, dietary, and moral instructions for the people, which became codified in the Books of Exodus and Leviticus as "the Law." Once the full Law had been received, the cloud of God's guidance lifted and the Israelites continued their journey.

The giving of the Law invested Shavuot with much deeper significance than that of the ancient wheat harvest by tying it in with the exodus and the establishment of a binding covenant between God and Israel in the Torah. Further confirmeation came after Jesus' ascension with the outpouring of the Holy Spirit, quickening the *logos* or written word of the law, making it lively and active as the *rhema* or living Word of God, and reminding us that the letter of the Law is dead without the underlying Spirit of God bringing it to life.

Celebration in the Faith Community

Shavuot or Pentecost is one of the holidays on which both *Hallel* or Psalms of Praise are recited and *Yizkor*, the memorial service, is observed in the Jewish community. The special readings for the holiday include medieval poems (*piyyutim*) and the Book of Ruth. The story of Ruth is recounted for many reasons, including that the book takes place at the time of the wheat harvest, that Ruth's assumption of Naomi's faith reflects the Israelites' acceptance of the Torah at Sinai, and that King David, who is alleged to have died at this time of year according to rabbinic tradition, is mentioned at the end of Ruth. Shavuot is a joyous time since it commemorates the moment at which God and Israel entered into a figurative marriage with each other, the hopeful springtime of their relationship. It carries the same message to the Christian community as it commemorates the birth of the church (*ekklesia* or "called out ones") through the timely outpouring of the Holy Spirit which quickened God's Word and propelled it into the entire world.

A Providential Occurrence

A significant part of the traditional Shavuot remembrances passed down for millennia involves participating on the eve of Shavuot in an all-night prayer meeting, a *Tikkun Leil Shavuot* of study and repentance for Israel's initial lack of faith as recorded in Exodus 20 below. Following the Tikkun Leil Shavuot tradition, the disciples of Jesus were gathered in Jerusalem for Shavuot with Jews from all over the civilized world and were observing this time of prayer when the Holy Spirit was poured out in their midst.

> *Moses said to the people, "Do not fear, for God has come to test you, that the fear of him may be before you, that you may not sin."* ***The people stood far off****, while Moses drew near to the thick darkness where God was.*
>
> Exodus 20:20-21

> *When the day of Pentecost arrived, they were all together in one place. And suddenly there came from heaven a sound like a mighty rushing wind, and it filled the entire house where they were sitting.*
>
> Acts 2:1-2

TISHA B'AV באב תשעה and TESHUVAH תשובה
40 Days of Repentance

Two months after Shavuot during the summer month of Av, the Jewish community observes a solemn day of fasting, lamentation, and mourning known as *Tisha B'Av* (באב תשעה or "the 9th of Av") to commemorate "Five Calamities" that beset the Jewish people historically. In addition to the destruction of both Solomon's Temple by Nebuchadnezzar in 586 BCE and the Second Temple by the Romans in 70 CE, several other major calamities which have befallen the Jewish people are included with even more being added as time has gone by.

In many ways Tisha B'Av – the "saddest day on the calendar" – raises the question "Why has all this happened to us?" and leads three weeks later on Elul 1 into a 40-day season of fasting and soul-searching prayer for conviction and genuine repentance called *Teshuvah*, meaning "to turn" or "return" to God. 30 days into this period the shofar of Rosh Hashanah sounds, warning penitents that their time is running out and that only 10 "Days of Awe" remain within which to repent. Teshuvah's "40 Days of Repentance" come to a close on Tishri 10 with "The Day of Atonement" or Yom Kippur as described in the following pages.

ROSH HASHANAH ראש השנה
"Head of the Year"

Celebration of *Rosh Hashanah*, the Jewish New Year (ראש השנה or "Head of the Year" in Hebrew), begins each fall on the first day of Tishri and lasts for two days. There are four "new years" in the Jewish year, one each for people, trees, kings, and animals. Because it marks the completion of the creation of the world in Jewish oral tradition and is the new year of people and legal contracts, Rosh Hashanah is considered the "*head*" even though the holiday actually takes place in the seventh month on the Hebrew calendar.

The Jewish High Holy Days, or *Yamim Noraim* (ימים נוראים or "Days of Awe"), start with Rosh Hashanah which is followed 10 days later by Yom Kippur, the "Day of Atonement." The Mishnah or "oral Torah" published in the second century CE refers to Rosh Hashanah as the "Day of Judgment," since it is believed that God opens the Book of Life on this day and begins to decide who shall live and who shall die. The days between Rosh Hashanah and Yom Kippur are viewed as an opportunity for Jews to "repent" (*teshuvah* or תשובה in Hebrew, which literally means "return" to God) in order to ensure a good fate.

Jewish people traditionally gather in synagogues on Rosh Hashanah for extended services that follow the liturgy of a special cyclical prayer book called a *machzor* (מחזור or "cycle") used during the Days of Awe. At specific times throughout the service, a *shofar* (שופר or ram's horn) is blown. The *mitzvah* (מצוה or commandment) to hear the shofar, a literal and spiritual wake-up call, is special to this time of year.

Jewish New Year is the only holiday that is observed for two days by all Jews (other holidays are observed for just one day within the Land of Israel) as it is also the only major holiday that falls on a new moon.

A common greeting on Rosh Hashanah is *shanah tovah u'metukah* (שנה טובה ומתוקה or "a good and sweet new year"). Many traditional foods for Rosh Hashanah – pomegranates, apples, honey, raisin challah, and honey cake – are eaten, in part, for their sweetness.

God's Appointed Times

YOM KIPPUR יום כפור
The Day of Atonement

In the seventh month, on the tenth day of the month, you shall afflict yourselves and shall do no work... For on this day shall atonement be made for you to cleanse you. You shall be clean before the L<small>ORD</small> from all your sins. Leviticus 16.29-30

Yom Kippur occurs on the 10th day of Tishri at the close of the High Holy Days ("Days of Awe") season that opened with Rosh Hashanah and is probably the most important holiday of the Jewish year. Many Jews who do not observe any other Jewish custom will refrain from work, fast and/or attend synagogue services on this day. As noted above, the holiday was first instituted in Leviticus 16 and then included with the others in Leviticus 23:26-32.

The name *Yom Kippur* means "Day of Atonement" and clearly explains what the holiday is about. It is a day set aside to "*afflict yourselves*" to atone for the sins of the past year. According to tradition, in Days of Awe all of our names are inscribed in "books" kept by God. On Yom Kippur, the judgment entered in these books is sealed.

Essentially, this day is put forward as your last appeal, your last chance to change God's judgment by receiving His conviction, repenting, and making amends. However, Yom

Kippur atones only for sins between man and God, not for sins against another person. To atone for sins against another person, you must seek reconciliation with that person as soon as you can, righting the wrongs you committed against them before Yom Kippur, if at all possible or appropriate.

Yom Kippur is kept as a complete Sabbath. No work can be performed on that day, and observant people are required to refrain from eating and drinking (even water), washing and bathing, and engaging in sexual relations. It is a complete, 25-hour fast beginning before sunset on the evening before Yom Kippur and ending after nightfall on the day of Yom Kippur. Much of the holiday is spent in the synagogue in prayer. In Orthodox synagogues, services begin early in the morning after the sun has risen and continue until mid-afternoon. People then usually go home for a late afternoon nap and return for early evening services which end at nightfall with the *tekiah gedolah*, a long blast on the shofar.

On Yom Kippur it is customary to wear either special priestly white garments or a *kittel*, the white robe in which the dead are buried, to symbolize the sacrificial purification of the temple, which is now identified with our body, and call to mind the promise in Isaiah 1:18 that "*though your sins are like scarlet, they shall be as white as snow.*"

As we look at the sweep of Biblical commemorations from Passover through Pentecost and culminating in Sukkot up ahead, we recognize a clear pattern. All three Pilgrimage Festivals are related to God's call through Moses to those who hear His voice to obey Him, leave their bondage, and journey to the Promised Land. Passover, celebrates God's sovereign and complete salvation of His people. The second festival, Shavuot or Pentecost, rejoices in His investment in them of His Word and the power of His Holy Spirit.

And the third, Sukkot (with Teshuvah, Rosh Hashanah, and Yom Kippur as associated preliminaries), reminds us of the thorough cleansing, purging work God does in releasing and sanctifying His people as they journey as pilgrims through wilderness hardships. For it is only through trials and tribulations that they learned and we now learn how to appreciate and apply His faithful provision in substance, Word, and Spirit in becoming His children.

God's Appointed Times

SUKKOT סוכות
The Feast of Booths or Tabernacles

Every fall following Rosh Hashanah, the High Holidays ("Days of Awe"), and the solemn fast and deep contemplations of Yom Kippur, we enter on one of our faith's most lasting and ongoing celebrations, Sukkot or the Feast of Tabernacles.

Each biblical holiday given to the Jewish people has these three aspects: God's people are instructed to observe the holiday in the present in order to remember something God has done in the past as well as discover some future prophetic purpose hidden within each festival. Thus Jewish people begin Shabbat each week by lighting of two candles, which stand for "Keep" and "Remember." In so doing, they remember how God rested on the seventh day of Creation while also looking forward to the millennial rest promised for the whole earth. Similarly, Passover and Pentecost look back on the Exodus from Egypt and the giving of the law at Sinai, while Christians believe that their hidden prophetic purposes were fulfilled in the resurrection of Jesus and outpouring of the Holy Spirit fifty days later.

The third annual pilgrimage festival, Sukkot, is a time when many of God's people gather in Jerusalem and around the world to commemorate His faithful provision for our spiritual ancestors as they journeyed in the desert from Egypt to the Promised Land and camped in temporary dwellings, called *sukkot* (Hebrew for "huts" – booths or tabernacles).

> *"On the fifteenth day of the seventh month, when you have gathered in the produce of the land, you shall celebrate the feast of the LORD seven days. On the first day shall be a solemn rest, and on the eighth day shall be a solemn rest... and you shall rejoice before the LORD your God seven days... All native Israelites shall dwell in booths, that your generations may know that I made the people of Israel dwell in booths when I brought them out of the land of Egypt: I am the LORD your God."* Leviticus 23:39..43

Sukkot also reminds us of the process of purification through trial that we all must go through after being called out of slavery to sin, empowered by God's Word and Spirit, and drawn closer to Him in love and trust as we prepare for and look ahead to the prophesied Messianic age when all the nations will flow to the New Jerusalem to worship the LORD.

Then the survivors from all the nations that have attacked Jerusalem will go up year after year to worship the King, the LORD Almighty, and to celebrate the Festival of Tabernacles. If any of the peoples of the earth do not go up to Jerusalem to worship the King, the LORD Almighty, they will have no rain.
                                                                        Zechariah 14:16-17

The solemnity of Rosh Hashanah and Yom Kippur yield every year to the joy of Sukkot as people erect temporary ceremonial shelters on their land and meet with loved ones to celebrate. In the reestablished State of Israel, festivities abound, including the annual festival of reconciliation hosted by the International Christian Embassy in Jerusalem. Scholars like Edward Chumney have noted that the birth of Jesus was on the first day of Sukkot, followed by His circumcision on the eighth day, celebrated as Shemini Atzeret.

SHEMINI ATZERET עצרת שמיני
Eighth Day of Sukkot

As its name indicates, this day immediately follows the seven-day observance of Sukkot and wraps up the fall pilgrimage festival with a gathering and celebration of gratitude for God's grace and provision. Prayer is offered for continuing favor (rain) on upcoming crops. John 7:37-38 reports that *on the last day of the [Sukkot] feast, the great day, Jesus stood up and cried out, "If anyone thirsts, let him come to me and drink. Whoever believes in me, as the Scripture has said, 'Out of his heart will flow rivers of living water.'"*

SIMCHAT TORAH תורה שמחת
"Rejoicing of the Torah"

The traditional observance of Simchat Torah is held in Israel on the same day as Shemini Atzeret. Elsewhere it usually occurs on the following day when the yearly cycle of Torah reading ends and the scroll is rolled back to Genesis again. Torah scrolls are removed from the ark and carried around inside the synagogue seven times in a joyful procession, often followed by children waving flags. There is singing and dancing and, for the children, sweets. The characteristic rejoicing of Simchat Torah expresses the joy that believers feel in their possession and observance of the words of the Torah (the "Law").

  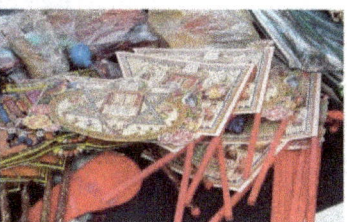

God's Appointed Times

HANUKKAH חנוכה
A Festival of Lights or Feast of Dedication

What is Hanukkah?

Hanukkah ("dedication" in Hebrew), also referred to as the Festival of Lights or the Feast of Dedication, is an eight-day holiday that celebrates the rededication of the Jerusalem temple in 164 BCE.

Historically, in 175 BCE Antiochus Epiphanes became ruler of the Seleucid Empire. His goal was to unite the Greek-related elements of his empire and to force, if necessary, those who did not live their lives based on Greek culture (e.g. those in Judea) to do so. In 167 BCE he ordered that a pagan altar dedicated to Zeus be placed inside the temple in Jerusalem. Unclean animals like pigs were ordered to be sacrificed on the new altar.

A small army of Jews known as the Maccabees rebelled, regained control over the Temple, removed the symbols of Zeus, and rebuilt a new altar to offer sacrifices in keeping with Jewish law. According to legend a miracle occurred at this time. There was only enough pure oil to keep the Temple's menorah, one of its most important ritual objects, burning for one day. But the flame stayed alight for eight days until a new supply of oil could be found, forming the basis for the eight-day celebration of Hanukkah.

Religious Observance

Although there are a variety of games like playing dreidel, special foods, gift giving, and enjoyable events associated with Hanukkah, the only religious observance related to the holiday is the eight-day ceremony of lighting of candles in commemoration of the miracle of the multiplying of the oil. The candles are arranged in a candelabrum called a menorah that holds nine candles: one for each night, plus a *shammus* (servant) at a different height.

Christmas timing

As noted above, scholars indicate that Jesus was born at Sukkot (which would suggest that conception took place during the Festival of Lights). However, during the reign of Roman Emperor Constantine in 336 CE and in keeping with a "replacement theology" movement to separate the celebrations of Christendom entirely from their Hebraic roots, December 25 was instituted as the day to celebrate Jesus' birth. Since the annual eight-day Hanukkah festivities start on Kislev 25 in the lunar-based Jewish calendar, Hanukkah's place in the civil calendar falls sometime at the end of our year where it often overlaps Christmas.

TU B'SHEVAT ט״ו בשבט
"New Year of the Trees" or Jewish Arbor Day

What is Tu B'Shevat?

Although not specifically established as a holiday in the Bible, the 15th of Shevat marks the beginning of a "new year" for trees and helps determine their age for being tithed according to Leviticus 19:23-24 and 27:30. Deuteronomy 20:19 also encourages us to honor and preserve trees, especially fruit trees, as part of God's provision. Tu B'Shevat usually occurs in either late January or February when the earliest-blooming trees in the Land of Israel emerge from their winter sleep and begin a new fruit-bearing cycle.

The date is marked by eating fruit, particularly from the kinds that are singled out by the Torah in its praise of the bounty of the Holy Land:

What Do People Do?

Many Jewish people, particularly in Israel and on kibbutzim, plant trees. The day is often marked at home by sharing a symbolic meal with family members and close friends consisting of dried fruit and nuts like grapes, figs, pomegranates, olives and dates, accompanied by red wine or grape juice. Some people also pickle or candy the *etrog* (a citrus fruit) used at the ceremonies during Sukkot and eat it on Tu B'Shevat.

God's Appointed Times

PURIM פורים
The Feast of Lots

Story of Purim in the Megillah of Esther

Purim is one of the most joyous and fun holidays on the Jewish calendar. It commemorates a time when the Jewish people living in Persia were saved from extermination.

The Book of Esther

The story of Purim is told in the Biblical book (scroll or *megillah*) of Esther with more details and commentary, often humorous, in the Babylonian Talmud (see Megillah 7b). The heroes of the story are Esther, a beautiful young Jewish woman living in Persia, and her older cousin Mordecai, who raised her as if she were his daughter. Esther was taken to the house of Ahasuerus, King of Persia, to become part of his harem. King Ahasuerus loved Esther more than his other women and made Esther queen, but the king did not know that Esther was a Jew because Mordecai told her not to reveal her identity.

The villain of the story is Haman, an arrogant, egotistical advisor to the king. Haman hated Mordecai because Mordecai refused to bow down to Haman, so Haman plotted to destroy the Jewish people. In a speech that is all too familiar to Jews, Haman told the king,

> *There is a certain people scattered abroad and dispersed among the peoples in all the provinces of your kingdom. Their laws are different from those of every other people, and they do not keep the king's laws, so that it is not to the king's profit to tolerate them.*
>
> Esther 3:8

The king gave the fate of the Jewish people to Haman, to do as he pleased to them. Haman planned to exterminate all of the Jews. The word "Purim" means "lots" and refers to the lottery that Haman used to choose the date for the massacre. Mordecai persuaded Esther to speak to the king about Haman's plot on behalf of the Jewish people. This was a very risky thing for her to do, because anyone who came into the king's presence without being summoned could be put to death, and she had not been summoned. Esther fasted for three days to prepare herself, then went in to the king. He welcomed her. Later, she told him of Haman's plot against her people. The Jewish people were saved, and Haman and his ten sons were hanged on the gallows that had been prepared for Mordecai.

The book of Esther is unusual in that it is the only book of the Bible that does not contain the name of God, due to fear of persecution. In fact, it includes virtually no reference to God. Mordecai makes a vague reference to the fact that the Jews will be saved by someone else, if not by Esther, but that is the closest the book comes to mentioning God. Thus, one important message that can be gained from the story is that God often works in ways that are not apparent, in ways that appear to be chance, coincidence, or just plain good luck.

Echoes of Purim in Our Era

The Pesach (Passover) Seder reminds us that in every generation, there are those who rise up to destroy the Jewish people, but God saves them from their hand. In the time of the Book of Esther, Haman was the one who tried to destroy the Jews. Ever since the time of Constantine, but especially during and after the Crusades in the 11th Century, Jewish people were often scapegoated and discriminated against grievously as "Christ-killers" and stubborn, perverse, and greedy infidels by substantial elements of the organized Christian and Islamic communities in the West. Much closer to our time there have been two major political cultures during the 20th Century who have threatened and persecuted the Jewish people in ways that bear an uncanny resemblance to portions of the Purim story.

Many have noted the echoes of Purim in the Nuremberg war crime trials. In the Book of Esther, Haman's ten sons were hanged (Esther 9:13); in 1946, ten of Hitler's top associates were put to death by hanging for their war crimes, including the crime of murdering 6 million Jews. An eleventh associate of Hitler, Hermann Göring, committed suicide the night before the execution, a parallel to the suicide of Haman's daughter recorded in the Babylonian Talmud (Megillah 16a). One of the men hanged, Julius Streicher, was keenly aware of the parallel when he shouted "Purim Fest 1946!" on his way to the gallows.

Another echo of Purim occurred in the former Soviet Union a few years later. In early 1953, Stalin was planning to deport most of the Jews in the Soviet Union to Siberia, but just before his plans came to fruition, he suffered a stroke and died a few days later. He suffered that stroke on the night of March 1, 1953, the night after Purim, and his plan to deport Jews was not carried out.

Purim Customs and Observances

Purim is celebrated on the 14th day of Adar, which is usually in March. The 13th of Adar is the day that Haman chose for the extermination of the Jews, and the day that the Jews battled their enemies for their lives. On the day afterwards, the 14th, they celebrated their survival. In cities that were walled in the time of Joshua, Purim is celebrated on the 15th of the month, because the book of Esther says that in *Shushan* (a walled city), deliverance from the massacre was not complete until the next day, which is then referred to as *Shushan Purim*.

The primary instruction related to Purim is to hear the reading of the book of Esther. God's people are also encouraged to eat, drink and be merry and to send out gifts of food or drink and make gifts to charity. A common treat at this time of year is *hamentaschen* (literally *Haman's pockets*). These triangular fruit-filled cookies are supposed to represent Haman's three-cornered hat.

Purim is not subject to the Sabbath-like restrictions on work that other holidays are, but some sources recommend not conducting ordinary business on Purim out of respect for the holiday. In fact, it is customary to hold carnival-like celebrations on Purim, to perform plays and parodies, and to hold beauty contests. In America Purim is sometimes referred to as the Jewish Mardi Gras.

Since Purim celebrations start on Adar 14 and Passover is exactly one month later on Nisan 14, the festivities of Purim bring us full circle in the Jewish calendar and prepare us to start another annual cycle of meaningful observances.

JESUS Ἰησοῦς or YESHUA ישוע ?

Why do we call Him Jesus if His Name is Yeshua?

By Mary Fairchild

A reader asks:

Jewish people say that our LORD Jesus' real Hebrew name is Yeshua. If it is true, then why are people worshiping him in the wrong name?

The reader is not the first person to ask this question. Some religious movements have argued that we worship the wrong Savior if we do not call him by his Hebrew name, *Yeshua* (ישוע).

Response:

He is correct in saying Yeshua is the Hebrew name for the LORD. It means "Yahweh [the LORD] is Salvation." The English spelling of Yeshua is "Joshua." However, when translated from Hebrew into the Greek language, the name Yeshua becomes *Iēsous* (Ἰησοῦς). The English spelling for Iēsous is "Jesus."

Basically, what this means is Joshua and Jesus are the same name. One is translated from Hebrew into English, the other from Greek into English. It is also interesting to note, the names "Joshua" and "Isaiah" are essentially the same names as Yeshua in Hebrew. They mean "Savior" and "the salvation of the LORD."

The Bible doesn't give preeminence to one language over another. We are not commanded to call upon the name of the LORD in Hebrew only. Acts 2:21 says,

And it shall come to pass that everyone who calls upon the name of the LORD shall be saved.

God knows who calls upon his name, whether they do so in Chinese, English, German, Hebrew, Russian, Spanish, or Swahili. He is still the same LORD and Savior.

What did Jesus look like?

People have a funny idea of what Jesus looked like. Jesus of Nazareth was not white-skinned. Jesus was not European. Jesus was a Jew. Jesus lived in the land of Israel, in the Middle East. The Bible tells us that Jesus walked wherever He went, so we can easily imagine that His olive skin would have been darkened by the sun.

Jesus would not have had a neat, trimmed beard, because a command (Leviticus 19:27) in the Law of Moses, which the Bible says Jesus observed, required Jewish males to *not round off the hair on your temples or mar the edges of your beard.*

Hundreds of years after Jesus' life on earth, artists painted pictures that made Jesus look handsome. They were not accurate representations of Jesus' likeness. The painters were following traditions and Western culture, rather than what the Bible says, and they certainly had never met Jesus. Sadly, their artworks continue to influence thinking to this day.

The only verse in the Bible about Jesus' physical form, before His death and resurrection, is found in Isaiah 53:2, which says:

> *He had no form or majesty that we should look at him,*
> *and no beauty that we should desire him.*

In other words, the only biblical description of Jesus during His time on earth says that He was not physically attractive.

Beauty, in God's eyes, comes from within.

Protestant   Evangelical   Catholic   Aryan   Hebrew

The Biblical Festivals

"Coat of Many Colors - LORD of All" by Thomas Blackshear

*This day shall be for you
a memorial day, and you shall
keep it as a feast to the L*ORD*;
throughout your generations,
as a statute forever.*

EXODUS 12:14

פסח סדר ההגדה בכתובים

A PASSOVER SEDER

THE TREE OF LIFE COMMUNITY
קהילת עץ החיים

BACKGROUND

The people of God have celebrated *Pesach* or Passover for thousands of years. Before the Exodus, the tribes of Israel celebrated a sacrificial festival in the early spring called *Hag HaPesach* (Feast of the Paschal Sacrifice), offering the firstlings of their flocks and herds to the LORD in thanksgiving for His tender loving kindness towards them. It was during this time of year, while the people of Israel were enslaved in Egypt, that Moses pleaded with Pharaoh for permission to hold this festival:

> *"The God of the Hebrews has met with us. Please let us go a three days' journey into the wilderness that we may sacrifice to the LORD our God, lest he fall upon us with pestilence or with the sword."*
>
> Exodus 5.3

Pharaoh refused them, and the sacrificial festival was transformed, as described in detail in the 12th chapter of Exodus, into the perpetual festival of deliverance that is celebrated each year by observant believers to this very day.

In Hag HaPesach animal sacrifices were offered out in the field, but in the Passover instituted by Moses, each family was commanded to sacrifice a lamb without spot or blemish outside their home in Egypt and to take the blood of the lamb and apply it over the doorposts of their house as a sign to all the powers in heaven and on earth that theirs was a household which believed and placed their trust in the living God, the God of Abraham, Isaac, and Jacob, and who were hearing the word of God for their age through His servant Moses. According to God's promise, when the Death Angel came through Egypt, striking dead the first-born sons of the Egyptians, he "*passed over*" those homes that were covered with the blood. In this way the host of heaven could distinguish between Egyptians and true Israelites: those who heard God's voice through Moses, believed in God, and obeyed His command were counted to be Israelites, while the remainder were counted as Egyptians. Since that time the Pesach feast has been known as the LORD's Passover.

The Passover meal is known as the *Seder* (סדר), which means "order" because the meal and service are done in a prescribed sequence. This sequence is presented in the *Haggadah* (הגדה or "telling") which outlines the steps of the meal as well as the readings and songs for the participants. While there can be a great deal of variety in how the service is conducted, the basic elements and order have remained unchanged for centuries. At various points in the service there are different actions required of the participants. All of the actions have carefully composed symbolic meanings, hence the Seder, the order.

Certain aspects of the Passover celebration are clearly outlined in Scripture, including advance preparations, the date and timing of the celebration, certain commemorative symbolic foods to be eaten during the Passover meal, and a special order to the narrative and ritual recounting of the Passover story. As the years have gone by, the feast has been refined in its structure and form with the elements carefully laid out in a Haggadah or storybook such as this one, which outlines the events and activities of the evening celebration.

Jesus was, and is, and always will be a Jew. During His earthly lifetime He was raised up in the Jewish practices and customs of His time and in the precepts of the Old Testament Scriptures. Since He was the living Word of God, His life was a fulfillment of Scripture. As we read of the words and deeds of Jesus' life in the Gospel accounts, it is striking to note how He became the fulfillment of the Passover, God's Paschal Lamb sacrificed for our sins, whose blood was shed that we, placing it over the doorposts of our hearts, might be spared from the Death Angel and enter into eternal life. On the night in which He was betrayed, Jesus celebrated a Passover Seder ceremony with His disciples in an upper room that had been prepared for them. During this special Seder, He took two of the Passover elements, the Afikoman and the Cup of Elijah, and consecrated them as the LORD's Supper, the Eucharist that believers have celebrated ever since.

The Seder outlined in our Haggadah is designed for believers both old and new who sense a call to observe the Passover feast as a remembrance of their own passage from bondage to deliverance, from slavery to freedom, through the mercies of the living God and the shed blood of the Paschal Lamb. Guests who are able to appreciate both the solemnity and the joy of our celebration are welcome to participate. As it has been written in Scripture,

> *In the first month, on the fourteenth day of the month at twilight, is the LORD's Passover… This day shall be for you a memorial day, and you shall keep it as a feast to the LORD; throughout your generations, as a statute forever, you shall keep it as a feast.*
>
> Leviticus 23:5 and Exodus 12.14

The Haggadah that follows was compiled from traditional sources and woven together with original commentary and selected additional Bible references. It was designed to be used at home, in small groups, or with larger gathering to celebrate the Passover. Over the years it has been enjoyed by many groups. Please receive and use it with our blessings!

PREPARATIONS and THE SEDER TABLE

Careful advance preparation by both hosts and leaders is a significant part of the joy of the holiday and key to having a memorable celebration. Location, guests, menu and recipes, and meal preparation plans all need to be decided and arranged in advance. Leaders should read through the Haggadah (at http://hiskingdom.us/times/passover/ with live links), and all participants are encouraged to read Exodus 12 and John 13-17 before the Seder.

The Seder begins at sundown with everyone seated at a beautifully set table, covered with a white tablecloth as a reminder of the bright sand of the Sinai desert and decorated in blue and gold with cheerful spring flowers and candles.

At the head of the table are arranged the special Passover elements listed below:

- A plate of three matzot, hidden under a cover or napkin, as a reminder of the unleavened bread the people of God carried as they fled Egypt.
- A wine goblet for use in ceremonial greetings throughout the Seder.
- A special ceremonial wine goblet, the Cup of Elijah, covered with a napkin and set out in a prominent place in front of the leader.

- The ceremonial Seder platter with six symbolic foods:

    1) Zeroah – The shank of a lamb, as a reminder of the Paschal lamb.
    2) Beitzah – A roasted egg, symbolic of the peace offering that accompanied the sacrifice of the lamb.
    3) Maror and Chazeret – Bitter herbs (and sometimes horseradish), calling to mind the bitterness of slavery.
    4) Haroset – a food made of apples and nuts mixed with wine and cinnamon to look like the mortar that the Hebrew slaves used.
    5) Karpas – Greens, parsley or watercress, to remind us of the promise of new life which bursts forth from God's bounty each spring.
    6) A dish of salt water into which the greens are dipped as a reminder of the tears shed by the slaves. Often on the side with horseradish on Seder plate instead.

- A bowl of water with a small towel for ceremonial washing.
- A small pillow on the leader's chair symbolic of the luxury of freedom, since slaves were not allowed to eat at their leisure while free men could dine comfortably.

Then, right at sunset after all have been seated, the ceremony begins…

A Passover Seder

דהההג בכתובים

פסח סדר

The Haggadah in Scripture

שבת נרות
LIGHTING THE CANDLES

Hostess while lighting the holiday candles:

Blessed are you, O LORD our God, Ruler of the universe, who has sanctified us by your commandments and commanded us to kindle the light of the holiday.

בָּרוּךְ אַתָּה יְיָ, אֱלֹהֵינוּ מֶלֶךְ הָעוֹלָם, אֲשֶׁר קִדְּשָׁנוּ בְּמִצְוֹתָיו וְצִוָּנוּ ל דְלִיק נֵר שֶׁל יוֹם טוֹב.

or in Hebrew (with vowel marks)

Leader:

In the beginning, God created the heavens and the earth. The earth was without form and void, and darkness was over the face of the deep. And the Spirit of God was hovering over the face of the waters.

And God said, "Let there be light," and there was light. And God saw that the light was good. And God separated the light from the darkness.

Genesis 1.1-4

Reader:

In the beginning was the Word, and the Word was with God, and the Word was God. He was in the beginning with God. All things were made through him, and without him was not any thing made that was made. In him was life, and the life was the light of men. The light shines in the darkness, and the darkness has not overcome it.

John 1.1-5

Leader praying:

O God, through your Son you have bestowed on your people the brightness of your light; Sanctify this new fire, and grant that in this Paschal feast we may so burn with heavenly desires, that with pure minds we may attain to the festival of everlasting light; through Jesus our Messiah and LORD.

People:

Amen.

קדש

1. KADESH – THE SANCTIFICATION

People:

Blessed are you, O Lord our God, Ruler of the universe, who has chosen us from among all peoples. You have sanctified and exalted us with your commandments. In love you have given us days of joy and seasons of gladness, even this Feast of Unleavened Bread, a memorial of our exodus from Egypt. You have chosen us for your service and caused us to share in the blessings of your holy festivals. Blessed are you, O Lord, who has sanctified Israel and the festive seasons.

Reader:

But you are a chosen race, a royal priesthood, a holy nation, a people for his own possession, that you may proclaim the excellencies of him who called you out of darkness into his marvelous light. Once you were not a people, but now you are God's people; once you had not received mercy, but now you have received mercy.

1 Peter 2.9-10

Reader:

One person esteems one day as better than another, while another esteems all days alike. Each one should be fully convinced in his own mind. The one who observes the day, observes it in honor of the Lord. The one who eats, eats in honor of the Lord, since he gives thanks to God, while the one who abstains, abstains in honor of the Lord and gives thanks to God. For none of us lives to himself, and none of us dies to himself. For if we live, we live to the Lord, and if we die, we die to the Lord. So then, whether we live or whether we die, we are the Lord's. For to this end Christ died and lived again, that he might be Lord both of the dead and of the living. Why do you pass judgment on your brother? Or you, why do you despise your brother? For we will all stand before the judgment seat of God.

Romans 14.5-10

Reader:

Therefore let no one pass judgment on you in questions of food and drink, or with regard to a festival or a new moon or a Sabbath. These are a shadow of the things to come, but the substance belongs to Christ.

Colossians 2.16-17

פסח סדר

The Haggadah in Scripture

Leader explains the four traditional Seder wine toasts to God (sanctification, deliverance, redemption, and acceptance) as presented in Exodus 6 below:

> *Say therefore to the people of Israel, "I am the LORD, and I will **bring you out** from under the burdens of the Egyptians, and I will **deliver you** from slavery to them, and I will **redeem you** with an outstretched arm and with great acts of judgment. I will take you to be my people, and I will **be your God**, and you shall know that I am the LORD your God, who has brought you out from under the burdens of the Egyptians."*
>
> Exodus 6:6-7

People while raising their wine cups together:

> Blessed are you, O LORD our God, Ruler of the universe and Creator of the fruit of the vine, who has given us life, kept us safely, and brought us to this holy season.

All drink the first cup of wine (the cup of sanctification).

ורחץ

2. URCHATZ – CLEANSING THE HANDS

Hostess brings in a small pitcher of water with a bowl and hand towel and pours water over the leader's hands.

כרפס

3. KARPAS – EATING THE GREENS

Leader takes a piece of the greens and dips it into the salt water. He then describes the symbolic meaning of the greens and salt water while distributing them to each person present.

People:

> Blessed are you, O LORD our God, Ruler of the universe, Creator of the fruit of the earth.

All eat the greens together.

יחץ

4. YACHATZ – BREAKING THE MATZAH

Leader takes the middle matzah out of its cover and breaks it in two, replacing one half between the two whole matzot and putting the other half in a wrapper as the Afikoman (Greek for *dessert*) to be shared at the end of the meal. While the Afikoman is being hidden the Leader discusses the origin of this ceremony and its significance for us today – the Messiah being broken, wrapped in a linen cloth, and then "hidden" in the grave, only to be found by those seeking Him later to complete the feast.

Reader:

Indeed, my servant shall prosper, be exalted and raised to great heights. Just as the many were appalled at him – so marred was his appearance, unlike that of man, his form, beyond human semblance – just so he shall startle many nations. Kings shall be silenced because of him, for they shall see what has not been told them, shall behold what they never have heard.

Who can believe what we have heard? Upon whom has the arm of the L<small>ORD</small> *been revealed? For he has grown, by His favor, like a tree crown, like a tree trunk out of arid ground. He had no form or beauty that we should look at him: no charm, that we should find him pleasing.*

He was despised, shunned by men, a man of suffering, familiar with disease. As one who hid his face from us, he was despised, we held him of no account. Yet it was our sickness that he was bearing, our suffering that he endured. We accounted him plagued, smitten and afflicted by God; but he was wounded because of our sins, crushed because of our iniquities. He bore the chastisement that made us whole, and by his bruises we were healed.

We all went astray like sheep, each going his own way; and the L<small>ORD</small> *visited upon him the guilt of all of us.*

He was maltreated, yet he was submissive, he did not open his mouth; like a sheep being led to slaughter, like a ewe, dumb before those who shear her, he did not open his mouth. By oppressive judgment he was taken away, who could describe his abode? For he was cut off from the land of the living through the sin of my people, who deserved the punishment.

And his grave was set among the wicked, and with the rich, in his death – though he had done no injustice and had spoken no falsehood. But the L<small>ORD</small> *chose to crush him by disease, that, if he made himself an offering for guilt, he might see offspring and have long life, and that through him the* L<small>ORD</small>*'s purpose might prosper. Out of his anguish he shall see it; he shall enjoy it to the full through his devotion.*

My righteous servant makes the many righteous; it is their punishment that he bears; assuredly, I will give him the many as his portion, he shall receive the multitude as his spoil. For he exposed himself to death and was numbered among the sinners, whereas he bore the guilt of the many and made intercession for sinners.

Isaiah 52.13 – 53.12
(Jewish Publication Society translation)

Leader associates the scriptural description of the Messiah with the form of the matzah, and then elevates the remaining matzot in their cover and says:

Behold, the matzah, the bread of affliction our fathers ate when they were slaves in the land of Egypt. Let it remind us of people everywhere who are poor, hungry, and separated from God. Let it call to our minds those men and women today who are still enslaved and without freedom. May all in need come and celebrate Passover with us. May God redeem us from all bondage and affliction. Next year at this season may all God's people and the whole house of Israel be free. And may all of mankind who are open and willing discover and enjoy the liberty, justice, and peace that we have found in the Messiah. Come, LORD Jesus!

מגיד

5. MAGGID – RECITATION OF THE SERVICE

Instructions

Leader begins by talking about the representative "four children" (wise, thoughtless, simple, and quiet) and the need to relate the Passover story in such a way that people of all ages and abilities can understand its significance. The Four Questions or *Ma Nishtana* (המ נשתנה) are recited, along with brief answers. The Recitation then proceeds to tell the story of God's dealings with the Israelites and Egyptians at the time of the Exodus, drawing parallels with the way God is dealing with His people and those who surround them in the world today. The Leader concludes by sharing about the finished work of the Messiah in fulfilling the Passover sacrifice by becoming our Paschal Lamb, and then may draw a parallel between God's judgment of Egypt and the coming judgment of the world.

Leader:

> Our Four Questions all relate to one big question: Why is this night different from all other nights?
>
> 1) On all other nights we eat leavened or unleavened bread. Why on this night do we eat only matzah, the unleavened bread? (The Israelites had to leave Egypt in a hurry before bread could rise.)
>
> 2) On all other nights we eat all kinds of herbs. Why on this night do we eat especially maror, the bitter herb? (In remembrance of the bitterness of slavery)
>
> 3) On all other nights we do not dip herbs even once. Why on this night do we dip twice, first the greens into salt water and then the bitter herbs into haroset? (To remember that the tears of the slaves have been replaced by sweet gratitude)
>
> 4) On all other nights we may eat at the table either sitting up or reclining. Why on this night do we recline? (In olden times free people reclined during mealtime, while slaves and servants stood and waited on them.)

The wine cups are refilled in preparation for a recitation of the Ten Plagues.

Leader:

> When Pharaoh defied the command of God and refused to release the Israelites, he brought judgment upon himself and his people, for the LORD afflicted the land of Egypt with plagues.

People:

> These plagues came upon the Egyptians because of their evil disobedience; yet we do not rejoice over their downfall and defeat.

Leader:

The Bible teaches that all people were created by God, even our enemies who would seek to destroy us.

People:

We cannot rejoice when any person needlessly suffers, so we mourn the loss of the Egyptians and express grief over their destruction.

Leader:

At this point in the service we spill wine from our cups at the mention of each of the ten plagues. Meditating upon the pain and suffering of these catastrophes, we cannot allow ourselves to drink the full measure. We express anguish that those who resist the will of God bring such terrible judgment upon themselves.

Each person spills out a drop of wine from his cup into a saucer at the mention of each of the plagues, a symbol of sadness that the victory had to be purchased through suffering.

People:

1) Blood. 2) Frogs. 3) Gnats. 4) Flies. 5) Cattle disease. 6) Boils. 7) Hail. 8) Locusts. 9) Darkness. 10) Slaying of the First Born.

Leader:

Is it for judgment that we praise God?

People:

No, it is for His mercies that we praise Him.

Leader:

Then let us praise God for His mercies.

People singing Song #1 "In the Presence of Your People" below* (or more complicated traditional Dayenu דינו †):

> In the presence of your people, I will praise your name,
> For alone you are holy, enthroned on the praises of Israel.
> Let us celebrate your goodness, and your steadfast love,
> For your name is exalted, here on earth and in heaven above.
> Lai, lai, lai, lai, lai, lai....

*Music: https://youtu.be/YMnp8F_U65Y
†https://en.wikipedia.org/wiki/Dayenu

A Passover Seder

הפסח סמלים
THE PASSOVER SYMBOLS

Leader while pointing to shank bone on the Seder plate:

This shank bone reminds us of the Passover Lamb, slain for our redemption. Just as the blood of the sacrificial lamb applied over the doorposts of their houses in Egypt assured our forefathers that the death angel would pass over them, so the blood of Jesus, our Passover Lamb, applied by faith over the doorposts of our hearts assures us that we have entered into eternal life in Jesus, our Messiah and LORD, and that the death angel will pass over us.

Reader:

For since the law has but a shadow of the good things to come instead of the true form of these realities, it can never, by the same sacrifices that are continually offered every year, make perfect those who draw near. Otherwise, would they not have ceased to be offered, since the worshipers, having once been cleansed, would no longer have any consciousness of sins? But in these sacrifices there is a reminder of sins every year. For it is impossible for the blood of bulls and goats to take away sins... And every priest stands daily at his service, offering repeatedly the same sacrifices, which can never take away sins. But when Christ had offered for all time a single sacrifice for sins, he sat down at the right hand of God, waiting from that time until his enemies should be made a footstool for his feet. For by a single offering he has perfected for all time those who are being sanctified.
Hebrews 10:1-4, 11-14

Reader:

The next day he [John the Baptist] saw Jesus coming toward him, and said, "Behold, the Lamb of God, who takes away the sin of the world! This is he of whom I said, 'After me comes a man who ranks before me, because he was before me.' I myself did not know him, but for this purpose I came baptizing with water, that he might be revealed to Israel." And John bore witness: "I saw the Spirit descend from heaven like a dove, and it remained on him. I myself did not know him, but he who sent me to baptize with water said to me, 'He on whom you see the Spirit descend and remain, this is he who baptizes with the Holy Spirit.' And I have seen and have borne witness that this is the Son of God."
John 1:29-34

Leader points to the matzah.

Reader:

This reminds us how, in the haste of their departure from Egypt, our forefathers had to take along unleavened dough. As we read in the Bible,

And they baked unleavened cakes of the dough that they had brought out of Egypt, for it was not leavened, because they were thrust out of Egypt and could not wait, nor had they prepared any provisions for themselves. Exodus 12.39

Reader:

Do you not know that a little leaven leavens the whole lump? Cleanse out the old leaven that you may be a new lump, as you really are unleavened. For Christ, our Passover lamb, has been sacrificed. Let us therefore celebrate the festival, not with the old leaven, the leaven of malice and evil, but with the unleavened bread of sincerity and truth. 1 Corinthians 5.6-8

Leader points to the bitter herbs on the Seder plate.

Reader:

This bitter herb reminds us of how bitter the Egyptians made the lives of our forefathers in Egypt. For we read,

And they made their lives bitter with hard service, in mortar and brick, and in all kinds of work in the field. In all their work they ruthlessly made them work as slaves. Exodus 1:14

In each following generation, every person who has been born of God is called upon to reflect with gratitude upon his deliverance from the bondage of the world. For we read in the Scriptures,

*You shall tell your son on that day, "It is because of what the L*ORD *did for me when I came out of Egypt."* Exodus 13.8

It was not only our forefathers that the Holy One, blessed be He, redeemed; He redeemed us too, the living, together with them.

Reader:

I consider that the present sufferings are not worth comparing with the glory that will be revealed in us. The creation waits in eager expectation for the children of God to be revealed. For the creation was subjected to frustration, not by its own choice, but by the will of the one who subjected it, in hope that the creation itself will be liberated from its bondage to decay and brought into the glorious freedom of the children of God. Romans 8.18-21

A Passover Seder　　　　　　　　　　　　　　　　　　　　　　　　ההגדה בכתובים

People with cups of wine uplifted:

> It is our duty, therefore, to utter thanks and prayer, to sing praise and adoration, to Him who performed these wonders for our fathers and for us. He led us out of slavery into freedom, out of sorrow into joy, out of mourning into festivity, out of darkness into light, out of bondage into redemption. We shall sing Him a new song, Hallelujah!

People set down wine cups and sing Song #2, "I will sing unto the Lord" (Exodus 15)*:

> I will sing unto the LORD
> For He has triumphed gloriously,
> The horse and rider has thrown into the sea. (Repeat)
>
> The LORD, my God, my strength, my song,
> Has now become my victory. (Repeat)
>
> The LORD is God, and I will praise Him,
> My Father's God, and I will exalt Him. (Repeat)

*Music: https://youtu.be/FwM4214SRYU

or as an alternate "A Shield About Me" (Psalm 3:3)†:

> Thou, O LORD, art a shield about me!
> You're my glory and the lifter of my head! (Repeat)
>
> Hallelujah! Hallelujah! Hallelujah,

†Music: https://youtu.be/5bUB3kT_ZOw or https://youtu.be/te7z-u80ZhQ

Reader:

> *There is none like you among the gods, O LORD, nor are there any works like yours. All the nations you have made shall come and worship before you, O LORD, and shall glorify your name. For you are great and do wondrous things; You alone are God.*

Psalm 86.8-10

Reader:

> *Great and amazing are your deeds, O LORD God the Almighty! Just and true are your ways, O King of the nations! Who will not fear, O LORD, and glorify your name? For you alone are holy. All nations will come and worship you, for your righteous acts have been revealed.*

Revelation 15.3-4

People singing Song #3 "Praise Adonai"*:

> Who is like Him, the Lion and the Lamb seated on the throne?
> Mountains bow down, every ocean roars to the LORD of hosts.

Praise Adonai, from the rising of the sun 'til the end of every day.
Praise Adonai, all the nations of the earth, all the angels and the saints sing praise.
(Repeat)

*Music: https://youtu.be/JG-R4DjBtog

or as an alternate **"Behold, God Is My Salvation"** (Isaiah 12:2)†:

Behold, God is my salvation, I will trust and not be afraid,

For the LORD my God is my strength and my song;
He also has become my salvation. (Repeat)
La, la, la . . .

†Music: https://youtu.be/Xpsr6VOnQEI

People with wine cups uplifted:

Hallelujah! Blessed are you, O LORD our God, Ruler of the universe, Creator of the fruit of the vine and Author of our redemption.

Everyone drinks the second cup of wine (the cup of deliverance).

רחצה

6. RACHTZAH – THE CLEANSING

Leader:

Now before the Feast of the Passover, when Jesus knew that his hour had come to depart out of this world to the Father, having loved his own who were in the world, he loved them to the end.

During supper, when the devil had already put it into the heart of Judas Iscariot, Simon's son, to betray him, Jesus, knowing that the Father had given all things into his hands, and that he had come from God and was going back to God, rose from supper. He laid aside his outer garments, and taking a towel, tied it around his waist. Then he poured water into a basin and began to wash the disciples' feet and to wipe them with the towel that was wrapped around him.

He came to Simon Peter, who said to him, "LORD, do you wash my feet?"

Jesus answered him, "What I am doing you do not understand now, but afterward you will understand."

Peter said to him, "You shall never wash my feet."

Jesus answered him, "If I do not wash you, you have no share with me."

Simon Peter said to him, "LORD, not my feet only but also my hands and my head!"

Jesus said to him, "The one who has bathed does not need to wash, except for his feet, but is completely clean. And you are clean, but not every one of you." For he knew who was to betray him; that was why he said, "Not all of you are clean."

When he had washed their feet and put on his outer garments and resumed his place, he said to them, "Do you understand what I have done to you? You call me Teacher and LORD, and you are right, for so I am. If I then, your LORD and Teacher, have washed your feet, you also ought to wash one another's feet. For I have given you an example, that you also should do just as I have done to you. Truly, truly, I say to you, a servant is not greater than his master, nor is a messenger greater than the one who sent him. If you know these things, blessed are you if you do them." John 13.1-17

Leader explains Jesus' actions during this part of the Seder and then couples may turn after reciting the following blessing and wash one another's feet if this is to be part of the ceremony.

People:

> Blessed are you, O LORD our God, Ruler of the universe, who has sanctified us with your commandments and instructed us concerning the washing of one another's feet.

מוציא מצה

7. MOTZI – GIVING THANKS and
8. MATZO – EATING THE MATZAH

Leader breaks the uppermost matzah and distributes while giving thanks for bread and sharing the significance of matzah as a symbol of our deliverance from bondage.

People:

> Blessed are you, O Lord our God, Ruler of the universe, who has brought forth bread from the earth.

> And blessed are you, O Lord our God, Ruler of the universe, who has commanded us to eat matzah.

Everyone eats the matzah.

מרור

9. MAROR – TASTING THE BITTER HERB

Leader discusses the meaning of the bitter herb and haroset while distributing or, especially if horseradish sauce is being used, pointing to some of each.

People:

> Blessed are you, O Lord our God, Ruler of the universe, who has sanctified us with your commandments, and commanded us to eat the bitter herb.

Everyone is instructed to eat a piece of whole horseradish dipped in haroset or move on to the custom below by making a "Hillel sandwich" with pieces of the undermost matzah.

כורך

10. KORECH – A REMINDER OF THE TEMPLE

Leader breaks the undermost matzah and distributes it along with the bitter herbs and haroset, then says:

> While the Temple yet stood, Hillel introduced a custom of his own into the Seder service: he would put together a piece of the Paschal offering, a piece of matzah and a piece of the bitter herb, and eat all three together, in accordance with the Scripture:

A Passover Seder   ההגדה בכתובים

They shall eat the flesh that night, roasted on the fire; with unleavened bread and bitter herbs they shall eat it.

Exodus 12.8

In this way he said that he could taste slavery and freedom at the same time. It reminds me of our human condition: it is easier to take the man out of Egypt than to take Egypt out of the man. Even after being brought to freedom, we still carry the marks of our former bondage within us that must be cleansed. So within each of us are traces of the bitterness of our bondage, sweet remembrances of our good works, and the unleavened bread of freedom in the walk in the Spirit.

Everyone eats the matzah, bitter herb, and haroset together.

שלחן עורך
11. SHULCHAN ORECH – THE PASSOVER MEAL

Hostesses set out Passover feast.

Leader offers a blessing.

Everyone enjoys the festive meal!

TRADITIONAL MENU

Appetizer: Matzo Ball Soup with Chicken Broth
Entree: Roast Brisket with Gravy or Stuffed Foul
Vegetables: Kugel (Potato, Matzo or Rice), Glazed Sweet Potatoes, Sunshine Carrot Coins, Broccoli, or Other
Garnishes: Matzah Rolls, Fresh Fruit, Haroset
Dessert: Coconut Macaroons, Carrot Cake, Date Squares, or Other

See Page 54 for recipes.

צפון

12. TZAFUN – EATING THE AFIKOMAN

After the meal, a search is conducted for the hidden (Hebrew *tzafun*) Afikoman. A prize may be awarded to "redeem" the Afikoman from the one who finds it.

Leader describes the significance of the LORD's Supper and then, holding up the Afikoman, says, "This we eat in remembrance of the Passover Lamb."

> *For I received from the LORD what I also delivered to you, that the LORD Jesus on the night when he was betrayed took bread, and when he had given thanks, he broke it, and said, "This is my body, which is for you. Do this in remembrance of me…" Whoever, therefore, eats the bread or drinks the cup of the LORD in an unworthy manner will be guilty concerning the body and blood of the LORD. Let a person examine himself, then, and so eat of the bread and drink of the cup. For anyone who eats and drinks without discerning the body eats and drinks judgment on himself.*

1 Corinthians 11.23-24, 27-29

Reader:

> *"I tell you the truth, he who believes has everlasting life. I am the bread of life. Your forefathers ate the manna in the desert, yet they died. But here is the bread that comes down from heaven, which a man may eat and not die. I am the living bread that came down from heaven. If a man eats of this bread, he will live forever. This bread is my flesh, which I will give for the life of the world."*

John 6.47-51

Leader offers invitation and prayer.

People share the bread of life.

A Passover Seder ההגדה בכתובים

ברך
13. BERACH – GRACE

Leader describes the third and fourth wine cups of redemption and acceptance, as well as the Cup of Elijah, and their combined and fulfilled place in becoming the LORD's Supper.

Reader: Elijah the Prophet

Now when John heard in prison about the deeds of the Christ, he sent word by his disciples and said to him, "Are you the one who is to come, or shall we look for another?" And Jesus answered them, "Go and tell John what you hear and see: the blind receive their sight and the lame walk, lepers are cleansed and the deaf hear, and the dead are raised up, and the poor have good news preached to them. And blessed is the one who is not offended by me."

As they went away, Jesus began to speak to the crowds concerning John: "What did you go out into the wilderness to see? A reed shaken by the wind? What then did you go out to see? A man dressed in soft clothing? Behold, those who wear soft clothing are in kings' houses. What then did you go out to see? A prophet? Yes, I tell you, and more than a prophet. This is he of whom it is written,

*"'Behold, I send my messenger before your face,
who will prepare your way before you.'*

"Truly, I say to you, among those born of women there has arisen no one greater than John the Baptist. Yet the one who is least in the kingdom of heaven is greater than he. From the days of John the Baptist until now the kingdom of heaven has suffered violence, and the violent take it by force. For all the Prophets and the Law prophesied until John, and if you are willing to accept it, he is Elijah who is to come. He who has ears to hear, let him hear."

Matthew 11.2-15

Leader holds up the uncovered Chalice and says:

This cup represents the blood of the Passover Lamb. *"This is my blood of the covenant, which is poured out for many," He said to them.*

Reader:

"This cup is the new covenant in my blood. Do this, as often as you drink it, in remembrance of me." For as often as you eat this bread and drink the cup, you proclaim the LORD's death until he comes.

1 Corinthians 11.25-26

Leader offers invitation and prayer.

People share in the LORD's Cup and then sing Song #4 "Holy unto You"* softly:

> *Chorus:*
>> Holy unto You, Holy unto You;
>> Hear this humble prayer and make me holy unto You.
>> Kadosh kadosh l'cha, Kadosh kadosh l'cha;
>> Hear this humble prayer, make me kadosh kadosh l'cha.
>
> *Verse 1:*
>> LORD I come to You, with a humble heart,
>> Seeking more of You, wanting less of me, wanting more of You.
>> From my deepest parts, God of mercy hear,
>> Comes an urgent prayer that my heart's desire is to You draw near.
>
> *Verse 2:*
>> I give myself to You, on the altar lay;
>> Spirit come and fill, so that I can more follow and obey.
>> Let Your light more shine, in this wounded heart;
>> Clean and purify, so that You can more of Yourself impart.
>
>> *Music: https://youtu.be/cV7VRt5FGdw or https://youtu.be/YW69sxYrf8I
>> Lyrics with chords: https://messianicchords.com/ChordSheets/1743

Leader praying:

> O God, whose wonderful deeds of old shine forth even to our own day; you once delivered by the power of your mighty arm your chosen people from slavery under Pharaoh, to be a sign for us of the salvation of all nations through faith in our Messiah: Grant that all the peoples of the earth may be numbered among the offspring of Abraham, and rejoice in the inheritance of Israel, through Jesus our Messiah and LORD.

People:

> Amen.

People singing Song #5, "Resting Place"*:

> *Verse:*
>> Heaven is my throne and earth is my footstool
>> Where is the house You will build for me?
>> Whom of You will hear the cry of my heart?
>> Where will my resting place be?

A Passover Seder

Chorus:
> Here oh LORD have I prepared for You a home
> Long have I desired for You to dwell
> Here oh LORD have I prepared a resting place
> Hear oh LORD I wait for You alone

>> *Music: https://youtu.be/AbLPdZldTRQ

or as an alternate "El Shaddai"†:

Chorus 1:
> El shaddai, el shaddai, El-elyon na adonia
> Age to age You're still the same by the power of the name
> El shaddai, el shaddai, Erkamka na adonai
> We will praise and lift You high, El shaddai

Verse 1:
> Through Your love and through the ram, You saved the son of Abraham
> Through the power of Your hand, turned the sea into dry land
> To the outcast on her knees, You were the God who really sees
> And by Your might, You set Your children free

Repeat Chorus 1

Verse 2:
> Through the years you've made it clear, that the time of Christ was near
> Though the people couldn't see, what messiah ought to be
> Though Your word contained the plan, they just could not understand
> Your most awesome work was done, through the frailty of Your son

Chorus 2:
> El shaddai, el shaddai, El-elyon na adonai
> Age to age You're still the same by the power of the name
> El shaddai, el shaddai, Erkamka na adonai
> I will praise You till I die, El shaddai (repeat)

>> †Music: https://youtu.be/tLM48ySdIDw

הלל

14. HALLEL – PRAISE THE LORD

Leader:

"Behold, I am coming soon! My reward is with me, and I will give to everyone according to what he has done. I am the Alpha and Omega, the First and Last, the Beginning and the End.

"Blessed are those who wash their robes, that they may have the right to the tree of life and may go through the gates into the city. Outside are the dogs, those who practice magic arts, the sexually immoral, the murderers, idolaters and everyone who loves and practices falsehood.

"I, Jesus, have sent my angel to give you this testimony for the churches. I am the Root and the offspring of David, and the Bright Morning Star."

The Spirit and bride say, "Come!" And let him who hears say, "Come!"

Whoever is thirsty, let him come; and whoever wishes, let him take the free gift of the water of life…

He who testifies to these things says, "Yes, I am coming soon."

Revelation 22.12-21

People:

Amen. Come, LORD Jesus.

Leader:

The Grace of the LORD Jesus be with God's people!

People:

Amen.

People singing Song #6. "I Exalt Thee" - Psalm 97:9*:

For Thou, O LORD, art high above all the earth;
Thou art exalted far above all gods. (Repeat)

I exalt Thee! I exalt Thee!
I exalt Thee, O LORD! (Repeat)

We exalt Thee! We exalt Thee!
We exalt Thee, O LORD! (Repeat)

*Music: https://youtu.be/xIZN0am96sE

or as an alternate "Immanuel"†:

Verse 1

A sign shall be given; a virgin will conceive;
A human baby bearing Undiminished Deity.
The glory of the nations; a light for all to see;
That hope for all who will embrace His warm reality.

Chorus

Immanuel, our God is with us.
And if God is with us, who could stand against us?
Our God is with us, Immanuel.

Verse 2

For all those who live in the shadow of death a glorious light has dawned.
For all those who stumble in the darkness, behold your light has come.

Chorus

Verse 3

So what will be your answer? Will you hear the call?
Of Him who did not spare His Son, But gave him for us all?
On earth there is no power; there is no depth or height that could ever separate us
From the love of God in Christ.

Chorus

†Music: https://youtu.be/O7DG3N6rYqk

נרצה

15. NIRTZAH – THE ACCEPTANCE

Leader praying:

May the thoughts of our minds and the meditations of our hearts be always acceptable in your sight, O Lord.

People:

Amen.

Leader:

Our Seder is complete. We have done all the things we were supposed to do. May we be free to enjoy a Seder like this one again – someday in the New Jerusalem!

People singing Song #7. "Hineh mah tov" (Psalm 133:1)*:

> Hineh mah tov uma nai im, shevet achim gam yachad!
> Hineh mah tov uma nai im, shevet achim gam yachad!
> Hineh mah tov, shevet achim gam yachad.
> Hineh mah tov, shevet achim gam yachad.
>
> Hineh mah tov uma nai im, shevet achim gam yachad. (Repeat)
> Hineh mah tov, hineh mah tov, Lai, lai, lai, lai, lai, lai, lai . . . (Repeat)

*Music: https://youtu.be/FkRgDPUyCLQ

or as an alternate "You Shall Go Out With Joy" (Isaiah 55:12)†:

> You shall go out with joy, and be led forth with peace.
> The mountains and the hills shall break forth before you.
> There'll be shouts of joy, and all the trees of the field
>   shall clap, shall clap their hands.
>
> And all the trees of the field shall clap their hands,
> All the trees of the field shall clap their hands (Repeat)
> As you go out in joy!

†Music: https://youtu.be/OH0XbpNY2g8

CHAD GADYA (AN ONLY KID)

Singing or reciting Chad Gadya (see illustration on Page 60) is an optional way to close a Seder celebration. Wikipedia notes that although it was a relatively recent (1590) and apparently upbeat addition to the traditional Haggadah, it is open to deeper interpretation.*

People singing† (or reciting sequentially around the table with Chad Gadya as a chorus at the end of each stanza):

Chad Gadya, Chad Gadya
My father bought for two *zuzim*
Chad Gadya, Chad Gadya

Then came a cat and chased the Kid
My father bought for two *zuzim*
Chad Gadya, Chad Gadya

Then came a dog and bit the cat
That chased the Kid
My father bought for two *zuzim*
Chad Gadya, Chad Gadya

Then came a stick and hit the dog
That bit the cat
That chased the Kid
My father bought for two *zuzim*
Chad Gadya, Chad Gadya

Then came the fire and burned the stick
That hit the dog
That bit the cat
That chased the Kid
My father bought for two *zuzim*
Chad Gadya, Chad Gadya

†How to sing:
https://youtu.be/iaZuI-WZTe8

Then came an ox and drank the water
That quenched the fire
That burned the stick
That hit the dog
That bit the cat
That chased the Kid
My father bought for two *zuzim*
Chad Gadya, Chad Gadya

Then came the shochet (butcher) and
    slaughtered the ox
That drank the water
That quenched the fire
That burned the stick
That hit the dog
That bit the cat
That chased the Kid
My father bought for two *zuzim*
Chad Gadya, Chad Gadya

Then came the LORD and He brought peace
Chad Gadya, Chad Gadya

Then came the water and quenched the fire
That burned the stick
That hit the dog
That bit the cat
That chased the Kid
My father bought for two *zuzim*
Chad Gadya, Chad Gadya

*According to some modern Jewish commentators, what appears to be a light-hearted song may be symbolic. One interpretation is that Chad Gadya is about the different nations that have conquered the Land of Israel: The kid symbolizes the Jewish people; the cat, Assyria; the dog, Babylon; the stick, Persia; the fire, Macedonia; the water, Roman Empire; the ox, the Saracens; the slaughterer, the Crusaders; the angel of death, the Turks. At the end, God returns to send the Jews back to Israel.

פסח סדר

The Haggadah in Scripture

TRADITIONAL RECIPES

Note: Conversion to Pesach

To convert recipes with regular flour for Passover, use the following formula:
1 cup flour = ¼ cup matzah cake meal + ¾ cup potato starch

Matzah Ball Soup

1 soup chicken	3-4 quarts water
Salt and pepper to taste	3 carrots peeled

Clean chicken and boil in water with carrots for 2-3 hours. Take bones and meat out and strain broth. Skim off fat. Serve the clear broth and the carrots with matzah balls. Celery and onions can be added. May need more salt after meat and bones removed.

2½ tbsps. chicken fat	
2 eggs	
¾ cup matzah meal	1 tsp. salt
1 dash cinnamon	¼ cup seltzer
1 pkg. sweetener	

Beat chicken fat well. Add eggs and beat again. Add liquid, seasoning, and meal to form a thick batter. Refrigerate for several hours. Boil water and roll into balls. Cook until they float. Let float, cooking for a few minutes. Add to soup broth.

Brisket

Marinate brisket in V8 juice – the longer the better. Cut up onions, carrots, celery and place on top of brisket before cooking. Roast with marinade and cover. Cook at 325° for 1 hour per lb. of meat. Puree veggies with marinade from pan, adding extra juice if needed, and serve as gravy over meat.

Matzah Meal Stuffing

Onion cut up fine. Sauté. Grate 3 carrots fine. Mix with 1½ cup broken matzah pieces. Add grated apple or water for moisture (no eggs). Salt and pepper to taste. Mix and stuff turkey or chicken.

Potato Kugel

6 medium potatoes	1 onion
1 carrot	¼ cup matzah meal
1½ tsp. salt	¼ tsp. pepper
2 eggs, beaten	¼ cup peanut oil

Pare veggies and either grate or put through grinder or food processor. Add rest and mix. Pour into well-greased 1½ qt. baking dish. Bake at 375° about 1 hour until tip is browned. Best to bake in a pan of water.

Matzah Kugel

 4 matzos   2 eggs
 ½ c sugar   2 tbsp. shortening
 ½ tsp salt   ½ cup raisins
 2 peeled, grated apples (optional)   lemon juice

Soak and crumble matzos, then let drip in colander. Mix all ingredients in an 8" greased pan. Bake at 325° for 40 minutes or more.

Rice Kugel

 1 cup uncooked or leftover cooked rice   ½ cup sugar (to taste)
 1 tsp. cinnamon   1 tbsp. melted shortening
 2 eggs   1 grated apple
 handful of raisins

Cook rice, rinse well. Add remaining ingredients. Bake in greased baking dish dotted with margarine for 1 hour or until nice and brown

Glazed Sweet Potatoes (serves 8)

 8 medium sweet potatoes   12 oz. jar orange marmalade
 2 tbsps. shortening   ¼ cup water
 ¼ tsp. salt

Boil potatoes until just tender. Peel. Cut in half lengthwise. In a large skillet mix marmalade, shortening, water, and salt. Bring to a boil. Add potatoes and cook over moderate heat. Baste and turn until glazed.

Sunshine Carrot Coins

 1 lbs. carrots thinly sliced   ½ c orange juice
 2 tbsps. fresh mint chopped or 2 tsp. dry   ¼ c raisins
 Pinch ginger and nutmeg   1 tbsp. orange rind
 1 medium orange, peeled and chunked   2 tsp. cold water
 1 tsp. Cornstarch

Cook first 6 ingredients, simmering covered about 8 minutes until tender. Add orange pieces. Mix cornstarch in water and add. Heat until thickened.

Matzah Rolls

½ cup water
1 tsp. sugar
1½ cup matzah meal
Garlic, onion or cinnamon

½ cup oil or shortening
1 tsp. salt
4 eggs

Bring water, shortening, sugar and salt to a boil. Lower flame. Add matzah meal gradually. Take off fire and cool. Add eggs one at a time. Shape into rolls with wet hands (make small because they spread). Bake at 400° for 35 minutes on greased sheet. Top with garlic, onion or cinnamon.

Ashkenazi Style Haroset

3 large, firm apples (core but don't peel)
1/3 cup red wine or grape juice
2-3 tsp. honey

1 cup walnuts, chopped fine
1 tsp. cinnamon

Grind or chop apples and walnuts. Add remaining ingredients and refrigerate for an hour or more.

Pesach Date Squares

1 cup dates, cut up
1 cup sugar
½ cup matzah cake meal

3 eggs
½ chopped nuts

Beat eggs with pinch of salt. Add sugar and beat well. Add cake meal, nuts and dates. Bake in greased 8"x8" pan at 350° for 40 minutes.

Passover Carrot Cake

6 eggs, separated
1 cup ground walnuts
1 tsp. vanilla

1 cup sugar
1 cup grated carrots
¾ cup matzah cake meal

Beat egg yolks 5 minutes. Gradually add 1 cup sugar. Beat 5 more minutes. Blend in carrots, walnuts and vanilla. Fold in cake meal. Beat egg whites until form still peaks. Fold into cake batter. Pour into 8" ungreased springform pan. Bake at 350° for 40-50 minutes. Invert pan on a cooling rack. Remove from pan when fully cooled. Sprinkle with sugar.

NOTES

JESUS FULFILLS THE

Hebrew Calendar		*Passover lamb observed for 4 days*				
Nisan Day	9	10	11	12	13	
Weekday	6th	Sabbath	1st	2nd	3rd	
Time of day	Thursday	Friday	Saturday	Sunday	Monday	
Twilight 9:00 pm		*Jesus eats with Mary, Martha and Lazarus* **John 12.2**	*Jesus stays in Bethany* **Matthew 21.17, 18** **Luke 21.37**			
Midnight	Friday	Saturday	Sunday	Monday	Tuesday	
3:00 am Dawn 9:00 am Noon 3:00 pm Dusk	*Jesus comes to Bethany six days before Passover* **John 12.1**	*Jesus enters Jerusalem* **John 12.12-15** **Matt. 21.1-11** **Mark 11.1-11** **Luke 19.28-31** *Israel selects their Passover lamb*	*Jesus teaches in Temple* **Matthew 21.23** **Luke 19.47** Israel "observes" the lamb they have chosen for three days		*Jesus sends disciples to find a place, arrives later* **Luke 22.7ff** **Matt. 26.17-20** **Mark 14.12**	
		Please study our Scriptural timeline of these events, which differs not only from current rabbinical interpretations but the post-Constantinian one we are so familiar with.				

Further Study

PROMISE OF PASSOVER

First Son	Feast of Unleavened Bread until Nisan 21			
14	15	16	17	18
Preparation Tuesday	Passover Wednesday	6th Thursday	Sabbath Friday	1st Saturday
Last Supper **Luke 22.13-16** *Gethsemane* **Matthew 26.36** **Luke 22.39**	*Regular Seder "Special Sabbath"* **John 19.31** **Leviticus 23.4-8**			**?** *Resurrection!* *Reshit Katzir (Firstfruits) and "Counting the Omer"*
Wednesday	Thursday	Friday	Saturday	Sunday
Jesus arrested **John 18.3** **Luke 22.53** *Priest's trial* **Matt. 26.57** *Pilate's court* **Luke 23.1** **John 18.28** *"King Game"* **John 19.1-5** *Crucified* **John 19.17-22** *Gives up spirit and is buried just before nightfall* **John 19.31** **Matt. 27.45** *Passover lamb is killed*	*Guard set at the tomb* **Matthew 27.62-65**		*Women rest on the regular weekly Sabbath* **Luke 23.56**	*Women come and find the tomb empty!* **Mark 16.2** **Luke 24.1** **John 20.1**
	3 days and 3 nights in the earth **Matthew 12.38-40**			

and Food for Thought

JEWISH HOLIDAYS 2022-2026 CE

Holiday	2022	2023	2024	2025	2026
Purim	Mar 16-17	Mar 6-7	Mar 23-24	Mar 13-14	Mar 3-4
Passover	Apr 15-22	Apr 5-13	Apr 22-30	Apr 12-20	Apr 1-9
Shavuot	Jun 4-7	May 25-27	Jun 11-13	Jun 1-3	Jun 21-23
Rosh Hashanah	Sep 25-27	Sep 15-17	Oct 2-4	Sep 22-24	Sep 11-13
Yom Kippur	Oct 4-5	Sep 24-25	Oct 11-12	Oct 1-2	Sep 20-21
Sukkot (First Days)	Oct 9-11	Sep 29- Oct 1	Oct 16-18	Oct 6-8	Sep 25-27
Simchat Torah	Oct 16-18	Oct 6-8	Oct 23-25	Oct 13-15	Oct 2-4
Hanukkah	Dec 18-26	Dec 7-15	Dec 25-Jan 2	Dec 14-22	Dec 4-12

"An Only Kid" (*Chad Gadya*) with two *zuzim* from The Rose Haggadah by Barbara Wolff

Further Study

ADDITIONAL REFERENCES

The Holy Bible
English Standard Version® ESV Study Bible™.

Rabbi Jim Appel
The Appointed Times Series.

Richard Booker
Celebrating Jesus in the Biblical Feasts, Expanded Edition.

Edward Chumney
The Seven Festivals of the Messiah.

Stephen Creme
Passover for the Rest of Us, A Guidebook on Celebrating a Passover Seder.

Erin Davis
7 Feasts, Finding Christ in the Sacred Celebrations of the Old Testament.

J. Hagemeyer
Love Feast, A Passover Seder Infused with the Gospel.

Barney Kazdan
God's Appointed Times: Understanding and Celebrating the Biblical Holy Days.

Susie Hawkins, Melanie Leach
Passover for Christians, Creating a New Easter Tradition.

Rose Publishing Series
Feasts of the Bible and *Christ in the Passover* - 2 pamphlets.

Jennifer Rosner
Healing the Schism.

Michael Strassfeld
The Jewish Holidays, A Guide and Commentary.

David Wilber
A Christian Guide to the Biblical Feasts.

Martha Zimmerman
Celebrating Biblical Feasts.

and Food for Thought

OUR SLAVERY PROBLEM AND GOD'S SOLUTION

What is going on?

From time to time our thoughts can get very big and far-ranging. What's the problem with people? In fact, what's the bottom line about our human condition? Why are we in such a mess? Then we take a deep breath and turn our attention back to more immediate issues, like what we should be doing right now.

But let's take a moment at the close of our experience with the Biblical festivals to let our thoughts expand and wander over the whole broad landscape of our common humanity. An overview like we've just gone through together goes way back in time, culture, and civilization to celebrate God's faithfulness to His chosen people in the broken conditions and situations they and we have found ourselves caught up in.

The difficulty with free will

Once we make the foundational assumption and confession that the God of the Bible – the God of Abraham, Isaac, and Jacob – exists and that He created us in His Image, we receive the key to understanding and overcoming our core problem, which is God's gift to us of free will. To exercise free will, we have to be allowed to make mistakes. And, having been put in charge of the choices we make, we inevitably end up making some poor ones.

Let's face it: no matter how much good we do, we're still imperfect and make one mistake after another, which has negative consequences for us and those around us. It can be really bothersome. We aim for the bullseye but miss the mark. Or we don't even know where the bullseye is and just aim in whatever direction feels right or seems to be the way to go in the moment. Or, imagine it, we shoot directly at what we've been led to believe is the target and hit its bullseye dead center, only to find out later that we were quite mistaken.

Basically, all we're really looking for is to have our own needs and those of the ones we care about met, and the most basic need we're hungering for is to be appreciated and loved. So when the going gets tough we try to meet these needs ourselves, often by seeking in the wrong places. We chase after money or things or emotional and physical experiences to comfort and encourage ourselves, and before you know it we're caught up in treadmills and rat races that just get us deeper in. For the sake of simple clarity, we can identify all of these human errors, large and small, with one time-honored word: sin.

The sad reality is that the burden of sin accumulates. Our parents were like this, and so were theirs. Our bosses and coworkers and neighbors and friends are all in the same boat with us. Along the way we pick up baggage – hurts, bad habits, things that trigger us and hold us back. And, as we wake up and begin to look around, we realize that all of us are mixed up in the same mess of human error – trapped there so to speak – and the pot keeps stirring. In another way of describing it, we're all enmeshed in and slaves to our own sin

Further Study

and the systemic effects of the sins of all those who surround us in time and space. Or, in even simpler words, we're drowning and lost in sin. God help us! How do we get out? Who will save us from these lives doomed to disappointment, frustration, and death?

A God-sized problem

Well, the condition we find ourselves in is certainly what could be called a God-sized problem. Fortunately for all of us the same God who made us, gave us free will, and knows us inside and out, has also provided us with a solution: a loving, ongoing, and working relationship with our Creator Himself.

For starters, He's taken the initiative in reaching out with a messianic plan to save us, as Isaiah prophesied millennia ago when he wrote, *All we like sheep have gone astray; we have turned – every one – to his own way; and the LORD has laid on him the iniquity of us all.* Read Isaiah 53 from beginning to end. You can start with the portion printed on Page 35. Then recognize the sacrificial character of God brought to human life in the person of His son and chosen Messiah, Jesus, and ask Him to rescue you and become your Savior.

Jesus knows all about humanity's problem in general and our version of it specifically. He's right at hand and ready to help us identify where we're mixed up, forgive us for the mistakes we've made, cleanse our hearts, and point us in the right direction. He cares about us and has the answers we need. He knows what's right at any given time and is able to communicate and share it with us whenever we're ready to listen. This is the God of the Bible that we celebrate in each of the festivals we've been studying.

Secondly, as soon as He's gotten our attention and commitment to participate in His plans, God has an amazing way of working out relationships and straightening out the messes we and others have made in our lives. We've gotten bent out of shape, bruised and broken, down and dysfunctional, but He will save and restore us if we will but yield to Him as LORD of our lives and cooperate with Him in mutual love.

Finally, He has great plans for us to work with Him in spreading the goodness of His Kingdom wherever we go, whether it's at home, in our communities, or in the broader world around us. All we need to do is keep asking, seeking, and knocking at His door, and then let Him lead and work with us in all we say and do.

Now it's your turn

What can and will you do with God's invitation? In the privacy of your life, call out to the God who saved the Israelites from slavery in Egypt, to the God who preserved Esther and her people, to the One who overcame evil plots, pushed back enemies, healed the sick, forgives sin, and illuminates the universe with His Word and Spirit. Receive Jesus as your LORD and Savior! Gather with the saints to grow in your love for God, sing the songs of the redeemed, and rejoice in your salvation! Hallelujah! Let's keep our own lifelong Biblical festival going!

and Food for Thought

OTHER HIS KINGDOM PRESS BOOKS

Celebrate Salvation® small group study guides in two Courses*

The Joy of Christian Discipleship Course 1
Established in 3 Stages and 7 Steps, a 36-week group study

1. **A - Saved!** *Rescued by Grace*
2. **B - Sanctified:** *Coming Clean with God*
3. **C - Sent:** *Becoming a Living Letter*

   Plus – Course 1 Handouts and Worksheets or **Complete Course 1**

Devotional Guide to 3 Stages and 7 Steps

4. **Essentials of the Christian Faith**
   7 Steps to Abundant Life, an 8-week daily devotional guide

The Joy of Christian Discipleship Course 2
Equipped IN 3 Realms with Understanding, a 36-week group study

5. **D - Awakening:** *The Triumph of Truth*
6. **E - Kingdom:** *God's Reign in our Midst*
7. **F - Heaven:** *Our Ultimate Destiny*

   Plus – Course 2 Handouts and Worksheets or **Complete Course 2**

---

* Information about and links to purchase all books as well as associated handouts in printable PDF form and other Additional Resources can be found online at https://celebratesalvation.org.

www.ingramcontent.com/pod-product-compliance
Lightning Source LLC
Chambersburg PA
CBHW081508040426
42446CB00017B/3437